HOW HIP HOP HELPED TO RAISE A GENERATION

Firstborn Malik

ISBN: 978-163901483-5

ABOUT THIS BOOK

How Hip Hop Helped To Raise A Generation is a look at the impact the golden era of Hip Hop played on the youth of that era. It's an eyewitness account of the lessons the children of that time were learning. This book also dives into the failures of the educational system to properly educate black youth. This book is educational, social-political, and thought-provoking.

CONTENTS

FORWARD

I will show how the Hip Hop golden era filled holes left by the school system. This book is a detailed account of the failures of the educational system. As you take this walk with me, I will explore various issues that affect our community. I will show you how conscious Hip Hop artists help to educate us. As I'm doing this, I will highlight pivotal moments in Hip Hop. I will show how rap artists of that era played a role in providing us leadership. Much of the work on this book was done through independent study. I did all the research necessary to produce a quality piece of work. I will help the reader understand the impact Hip Hop culture had on the youths of my era. I'm not a professor. I don't claim many degrees, but I have a wealth of knowledge from personal experience. I read many great books, and I can apply rational thought. I served in the United States Navy, so I got to see firsthand most of the world. I forged relationships with the people of the countries I visited to understand their culture better. I observed how people across the globe viewed blacks. I discovered that most of the negative images of blacks in America weren't shared by most people I met abroad. Some countries overwhelmed me with their love for black culture. My experiences felt similar to Miles Davis. In his documentary, he mentioned how well jazz artists were treated abroad while facing discrimination in the United States. When I was growing up, most of the images of black people were crafted in negativity. It was the era when so-called "blaxploitation" movies were popular. Around the time, black shows started to make it onto network television. Hip Hop artists helped redefine the black male/female image and even expanded on some. This book is about how Hip Hop helped raise a lost generation of black youth, i.e., the children of generation x, who were left devoid of leadership. Rap artists filled this leadership void, inspiring a whole generation of young people. Hip Hop's unapologetic urban appeal was intelligent, creative, inspiring, and controversial. I observed the impact Hip Hop was making globally. This era of Hip Hop was our black power movement.

I was raised in the B.W. Cooper, also known as the Calliope projects. Most of this manuscript was finished before August 29, 2005, the infamous date of hurricane Katrina. My original manuscript was destroyed; I had to redo everything because of that. This process helped me clear up some inaccuracies, and my views changed on some subjects. This is a quasi autobiography. It would have been impossible to write this book in the second or third person. I serve as direct evidence of everything I will present. I'm a child of that era when Rappers Delight was released; I was only eight years old at that time. Most of the topics I discussed aren't new to the black community. The difference is I will show examples of how some of us dealt with them in the Hip Hop movement. I will also give some solutions, but I will reserve most of them for another book, maybe in the future. Before I go forth with solutions, I want this book to serve as a positive dialogue platform. I couldn't do this book alone; it isn't just about me; it's also about my community, the village that played a role in developing me to be a man. It's about how Hip Hop helped to quench my thirst for knowledge. It's a story that many can relate to during my era. Creep with me as I show you HOW HIP HOP HELPED TO RAISE A GENERATION.

CHAPTER 1

IT'S YOURS.

"Commentating illustrating description given, adjective expert analyzing surmising musical myth seeking people of the universe this is yours." "It's Yours" T-La Rock.

When I was growing up like most children, my first glimpse of the world was through television. I watched numerous cartoons and television shows ignorant of the subliminal racism in some of them. I noticed the television shows that always featured white people embracing life. When someone was pregnant on The Waltons, All In The Family, or Little House On The Prairie, it was greeted as a joyous occasion. This would contrast with if someone got pregnant on Good Times, Sanford and Son, or What's Happening. What's Happening was about three brothers named Raj, Dwayne, and ReRun who lived in Los Angeles. They often hung out at Rob's Place, a restaurant in their neighborhood. There are all kinds of funny characters on the show, like Shirley, the waitress at Rob's Place, and Raj, little sister Dee. It was a positive show about friendship, and it didn't deal with many social issues. Good Times was a situation comedy about the Evans family who lives in the projects on the south side of Chicago. Good Times was one of the few television shows I could relate to.

**"I can relate to the Good Times, the Cosby's only sometimes."
"Ragtime" Brand Nubians.**

I recall an episode when a friend of Penny got pregnant. Penny was a character of the show made famous by Janet Jackson. Willona, her adopted mother, tried to distance her from the girl. She deceived Penny telling her the child had stomach mumps. In another episode, a sister decided to put her child up for adoption. This gave me the impression that black life is neither celebrated nor wanted.

I wondered why Laverne or Shirley never got pregnant or what would have happened if Chachi had knocked up Joanie? This made me aware of how afraid we are to educate our children on these matters. It's a contributing factor to why some black children grow up with low self-esteem. Including Good Times, other cool shows featured blacks like Sanford and Son, Different Strokes, and The Jeffersons. Sanford and Son were hilarious. The show starred comedian Red Foxx and Demond Wilson; this show was about a complicated relationship between a junk dealer and his grown-up son. Different Strokes was about Arnold and Willis Jackson, two black kids adopted by a wealthy white man named Mr. Drummond.

The Jackson's were the children of his maid that he promised to take care of after she died. This show was interesting: a rich white dude adopting two young brothers. I was amazed at how comfortable he was with these young brothers living under the same roof as his daughter. The Jeffersons was a spin off of All In The Family. Sherman Helmsley portrayed George Jefferson, a successful black man who owns a chain of dry cleaners in New York. He lives with his wife Louise in a deluxe apartment on the east side of town. This show was interesting; until then, I had no idea what an interracial relationship was. The only White people I ever saw were a few brave insurance men or the White Cat named Frankie that ran the corner store.

I didn't think Blacks and Whites married each other. Tom Willis was white, but Helen Willis was black. I wonder what the show would have been like if those roles were reversed? The Jeffersons had a witty black maid named Florence; she was the one that often stood up to Mr. Jefferson. Then there was Starsky and Hutch, my friends, and I really liked this show. The show was perfect; it was about two slick white cops who drove a flashy car, and what I liked most about that show was from a character named Huggy Bear, played by Antonio Fargas. I loved his persona, how he talked, and how he dressed. As children, we can get lost in television. The networks make these characters seem large. At those ages, children only can see superficially. Once I was older, I realized Huggy Bear was nothing but a snitching ass pimp.

It bewildered me how Good Times dealt with crime, drugs, teenage pregnancy, and unemployment; however, we never see those issues on the Brady Bunch, Eight is Enough, or Happy Days. When James Evans was killed in Good Times, the show became real to me. My father was killed, and my mama was a single mother of three in the projects. I enjoyed watching Sanford and Son, Good Times, and The Jeffersons, but Norman Lear cannot articulate black culture regardless of how great a writer he is.

A few years later, "The Cosby Show" came on the air. Immediately the show displayed a positive image of the black family. The show was about Dr. Heathcliff Huxtable and his wife Claire, a lawyer. These two black professionals live in New York with their five eccentric children. I was impressed with the Cosby show. Until then, I had never seen a black family portrayed in this manner, not even in the movies. Inexplicably some black people did not like the show. Some claimed they dislike the show because black professionals don't really marry each other. Others claim the children weren't typical black children or that no black family is that successful. I couldn't understand this; it fed into a negative stereotype.

Back in those times, most people in the community tried to have morals. There were neighbors my mother authorized to whip my ass if they caught me misbehaving. We had a lot of self-pride. Education was encouraged, and respecting your elders was normal. I knew we weren't rich, but at the time, it didn't seem like much of an impediment. Looking back, I don't know how my mama did it. We always had food, clothes and she kept a roof over our heads. Back then, my only worries were what games I would play with my friends or my daily chores.

The church is a traditional aspect of life in the black community. The church was always one of the places where we discussed ideas to help the community. My grandmothers tried their best to keep us in church. Church services were interesting. I was astonished at how the pastor commanded so much admiration. He gave out instructions read from his Bible and moved the congregation with his sermons. I dozed off in between some of them but, I was usually awakened by the shouts of people catching the Holy Ghost or an occasional nudge from my grandma. I paid attention to how they always collected money. I thought you couldn't go to church without it. I imagined that Jesus had to be rich with all the money collected on his behalf. My mama and grandma provided me money for the church that I sometimes would spend on candy or video games.

Like most families, holidays were important to us. I'm from **New Orleans.** We celebrated more of them than most people. **Mardi Gras** is a holiday for us, but for most people worldwide, that's just another Tuesday. We have **St. Joseph's** day and **"Super Sunday's"** which are unofficial holidays. On St. Joseph's day or Super Sunday, the **Mardi Gras Indians** prance around town. They adorned in some of the most beautiful Indian costumes you'll ever see. I've been told that they wear these costumes as a way to pay homage to the Native American Indians that took slaves in as refuge. Some Indians eventually had relationships starting families with these slaves. They make these suits annually, sewn by hand in great detail. There are brass bands and buck jumping crews who **second line** all over the city. The second line is a tradition unique only to New Orleans. The mainline is the brass band; the "second line" is those who dance and follow along. Some of these brass bands sometimes play at funerals.

As a child, these holidays were a source of analytical thinking. Let's take Christmas. I thought one man couldn't deliver presents to every child in the world in 24 hours. Regardless of how many elves he had to help him. I lived in the projects where we had no chimneys, so how was he getting these presents into the house? I have seen reindeer in the Audubon Zoo. They don't fly, nor do they Red Noses that light up like Rudolph's. I never question these inaccuracies because there were always rewards at the end.

Another holiday of interest was Easter. For this special day, we boiled eggs then dye them pretty colors. Some people even hide them and have Easter egg hunts. The churches are always crowded on this particular Sunday. Every year everyone always chooses this specific day to attend church. We all got new outfits, and everyone prepared a nice meal. The interesting part of Easter was the "Easter bunny," the mythical figure that laid the eggs we hid or dyed.

At that time, it never dawned on me that rabbits don't lay eggs. These two holidays represent the birth, death, and resurrection of Jesus Christ, but the Easter bunny and Santa get all the props.

Thanksgiving was another memorable holiday my mama would buy food weeks in advance to cook that day. I never understood the meaning of this holiday other than an occasion to overeat and watch football with your family.

Following Europeans, we participate in these holidays. No black culture is represented in any of them; Santa Claus is an overweight bearded Irishman.

The Easter bunny is a fictional animal, while thanksgiving involves white Pilgrims and Native American Indians.

Like every other holiday, Mardi Gras is also European. There's only one all black Mardi Gras organization or what they call krews. The **Zulu** organization is a predominantly black social and pleasure club (they allow white people to join now) that started in **1916**. Zulu's original members were disgruntled for being denied membership in any of the all-white krews. So they started one of their own then named it behind the famous African tribe. On Mardi Gras Day, Zulu members masked up in black faces and grass skirts. They stand on top of tractor-pulled decorated floats throwing Zulu's cherished throws. The most cherished of them all is the shaved-down decorated coconuts they are famous for. All the other Mardi Gras krewes are overwhelmingly white, like Rex, Bacchus, Endymion, Babylon, and Comus. The all-white krewes wear masks that resemble the klan's men. From top floats, they throw beads, doubloons, cups, coasters, and trinkets. It's insane considering black people be yelling, "Throw me something, mister." Some krews like Bacchus used to throw doubloons that would give you a free meal at Popeye's chicken. After a while, I was only interested in seeing the girls and the marching bands.

With all that's celebrated, any black child would wonder and ask where does he or she fit in? Everything celebrated in this country reflects people other than us. Most of these holidays originated from Europeans crafted in paganism.

My first real look into black history was through **Alex Haley's** mini-series **"Roots."** Roots were Kunta Kinte's story**, a Mandinka warrior** from **Gambia, West Africa**. As a part of his manhood training, he's sent out to capture a bird unharmed. While he's out trying to fulfill this quest, he's captured by slave traders. I used to hear people talk about slavery, but I had no idea what they were talking about. It was good to see something on television about it finally. I felt uncomfortable watching Roots at the same time

I was curious. Before Roots came on TV, white people had been portrayed as nice and wholesome. I was glued to the TV and watching what they were doing to all these innocent black people. It placed fear in me. Being afraid like that angered me in a way that weakens my soul. Roots affected me; until then, I never really paid attention to skin color. When the mini-series ended, slavery started to be discussed everywhere, including in school.

Then they started teaching us about something called **"Jim Crow."** Jim Crow was a set of racially specific laws enacted mostly in the south. I saw photos of black people protesting these unfair laws and watched videos of the police sicking dogs and spraying water hoses on them. Police officers beat black people for sitting down to eat at restaurant counters. Hooded white men called the Klu Klux Klan terrorized black people. I was taught to do like **Dr. King**. **"We Shall Overcome"** was the theme song of the struggle. I learned that any white person appearing sympathetic to black people was murdered, like **Abraham Lincoln, John Brown, Michael Schwerner, Andrew Goodman, Robert Kennedy,** and **John F. Kennedy**.

It was clear that white people were in power. I observed how we conducted ourselves around white folks. My grandma had a white insurance man; whenever he came over, she would speak and act differently. I can tell when my mother or grandmother talked to someone white over the phone by their demeanor. I found myself following behind the matriarchs by acting differently in the presence of white people.

My family successfully made life seem normal, but we were in the projects. I observed how people lived on St. Charles compared to someone living on **Martin Luther King**. It's disheartening that such a nonviolence champion has streets named behind him that people are afraid to walk on.

The community and the school play a big part in children's lives. This is no different in the black community. My elementary, junior high, and high school we're all blacks; we had no white or Latino children. We didn't even have children from the Caribbean, but we had a few courageous white teachers among the mostly black staff. I found school interesting regardless of what they taught. I thought the school could give me the answers I was searching for. I decided that I would remain a good student no matter what was going on.

I've always been a bookworm. When my mama recognized this, she took me to get a library card. I was excited to see that many books in one place. My next door neighbor Mrs. Helen also noticed my interest in reading. She was old enough to be my grandmother and one of the nicest people I ever met. All the children loved her. She was the head janitor at an elementary school. After 35 years, she retired from the Orleans Parish school board. I read her articles weekly from the States-Item, Louisiana Weekly, or the Times-Picayune. She bought me plenty of books. At first, she bought them fun with Dick and Jane books, Dr. Seuss, reader's digest, and World Geographic magazines. Later she bought me books from authors like Mark Twain, F. Scott Fitzgerald, and Charles Dickens. The most interesting book she ever bought me was a childhood bible. This Bible was special; it had all these beautiful illustrations of black people. At first, it scared the hell out of me, and I took it to be sacrilegious. I thought about throwing it away because all the images I ever saw of anyone in the Bible were white. This included those in the church and the walls in my family homes. Naturally, I assumed that the Bible people were white. I threw that Bible in the back of our junky closet. I was hoping that would release the demons. I hope never to see it again.

One day my mama got fed up with that cluttered up closet. She decided it needed to be cleaned. After school the next day, we spent all evening cleaning out that closet. We threw out a lot of stuff and then reorganized the rest neatly. We eventually stumbled upon that black Bible. My mama looked it over then decided we should keep it. So we left it neatly on the shelf with all the other books. I was overruled. The scary book will remain in the house. The next day I felt compelled to retrieve it, which ended up being a good decision. I read it constantly in awe of all the beautiful black characters. I got so interested in the illustrations without realizing I was learning the Bible. This brought new questions to my mind, and one of them is: if Jesus isn't white, why do they portray him that way? Like anyone involved in the church, I considered the Bible people to be righteous. I struggled with the concept of them being white because white people owned slaves. Other questions are: If white people are the Bible people, what made them turn so evil? What did our ancestors do to deserve such mistreatment? If the Bible people are black, how did we fall from grace? I learned that most of the geographical regions of the Bible were inhabited by black people, which increased my confusion. I wonder why these people are always portrayed as white.

School was a home away from home. We had lots of after-school programs with a few dedicated teachers. This gave us extracurricular activities keeping us off the streets. I hung out at **Rosenwald Park,** where I played baseball and football. Brothers like Coach Wayne, Coach Peanut, and Coach Terrell were important in teaching us teamwork, loyalty, and discipline. They provided us with the male role models that we all desperately needed.

The school was an interesting dynamic. I didn't realize that until the 3rd grade. I received good grades, but I didn't get any awards at the annual academic ceremony. I had a perfect report card, and my mama attended, anticipating that I would get recognition. She was proud of us when we did well in school. She loves sharing this information with family and friends. Unfortunately, my mama would not get to see what she had hoped for that day. I received no awards, and both she and I were left dumbfounded. There were a few days left before school officially ended. The next morning my mama awakened me. We got dressed then went to my school. Once there, she confronted my third-grade teacher Mrs. Butler asking her, "how come you didn't give my son any recognition?" Then she said, "I dare you to show me a better report card than his." She admonished her saying, "you should be ashamed of yourself for doing this to my son." I learned from that experience that my mama really was interested in my education. The whole experience taught me a lesson. I learned that sometimes when you do well, you may not be rewarded. After we left, my mama told me, "next year, you have to do better."

I discovered just how different black males were treated in school. Most of the awards went to the girls. Class participation was mostly aimed at females. Some teachers just considered black males a nuisance. Most of the discipline handed out went to the boys, although the girls were just as mischievous.

I grew up in New Orleans, where skin tone and hair texture play a role. If you were light skin with "good hair," you can get away with a lot. Punishment for your misdeeds revolved around your gender or skin hue. The darker you are, the more trouble you found yourself in. Skin hue has always been a division source; some of us are struggling with this issue, especially as children. This is something that we have no control over and are out of control about it. People in my family come in all shades; some can easily be mistaken as native, white, or Latino. Because of this melting pot of hues, I never had any issues. Unlike most dark skin brothers, my family ensured to make me feel special. My grandma, aunts, and cousins always made such a fuss when I came around. They often showered me with attention. They used to give me cool nicknames and compare me to successful dark skin brothers like Nat King Cole, Sidney Poitier, or Flip Wilson. Some of my friends asked me if my family treated me differently. Most of them were surprised when I said no. Some of my friends grew up in homes with siblings that didn't share the same father. Some had fathers with different skin hues this sometimes caused division. I've heard some sad stories, so I considered myself fortunate.

In my neighborhood, calling someone "black" was considered offensive. Uttering that to someone has led to plenty of fights. I found those insults ridiculous, considering my skin was something I couldn't change. If I found myself fighting about that, I would be fighting my whole life. This type of behavior is a clear indication of self-hatred—this mixing pot of psychological problems plagues black children. The seeds were planted before I was born.

My 5th-grade year was the most interesting year I ever had in school. This year was so interesting because my school had two 5th grade teachers **Mrs. Pittman** and **Mrs. Tolley,** a white woman. Mrs. Pittman was a well-known disciplinarian infamous for her paddle. My older brother was in her class. One day Mrs. Pittman caught him misbehaving. She gave him the paddle then instructed him to meet her in the bathroom. This was her usual way of issuing out discipline. That day, she forgot my brother was in the bathroom. He ended up staying there after school. This enraged my mama, so she went down to the school the next day and gave Mrs. Pittman the business. So on the first day of school, my mama came to school with me. She was determined that I would not be in Mrs. Pittman's class. This was embarrassing. It was the 5th grade; besides the usual ones, no other kid's parents were there. It felt like she was making me look special or something. The concept of having Mrs. Tolley as a teacher scared the hell out of me. I hated that I would have to behave a certain way around her. I thought I could be myself around Mrs. Pittman even though she was mean as a bull.

Just as my mama insisted, I was placed in Mrs. Tolley's class. This ended up being a blessing as Mrs. Tolley was a good teacher. She was one of the few teachers that were considerate of their students. She knew what all her student's strengths and weaknesses were. She helped us get better in any areas we were weak in while improving our strengths. Mrs. Tolley had an effective way of teaching. She was a great disciplinarian without being intimidating like most teachers. I loved her class, and I was one of her best students. She played a huge role in reducing my fear of white people, so I didn't feel the need to behave differently around her. This brought on a new line of questions. How could this white woman relate to us better than most black teachers at this school? Why is Mrs. Tolley nice even though she's Caucasian?

The funny thing was Mrs. Pittman, and Mrs. Tolley's classes were conjoined. A partition separated both classes in the middle that could be opened. Most teachers opened them only when we had parties or special events, but these two kept theirs open. They both shared responsibility for all the children, so technically speaking I was just as much Mrs. Pittman's student. When students got out of line in Mrs. Tolley's class, they got the paddle. I think Mrs. Pittman just got so busy and forgot my brother was in the bathroom. I doubt she harbored any ill will for him or my family, but I understand my mother's response. My 5th-grade year was the apex of my time at Sylvanie. At the end of the year, I received all the appropriate accolades my mama was thrilled.

That year we were supposed to go to middle school, but Orleans Parish added the 6th grade to my school. At the same time, my 5th-grade year was great.

My 6th-grade year was wack. My 6th-grade teacher Mrs. Coleman was horrible. She placed me in the back of the class with all the troubled boys. The way she mistreated young men in her class made me hate to go to school. To embarrass us, she scolded us in front of the whole class. I don't know how I managed to make decent grades in her class? I wanted to ask my mama to have me transferred to Mr. Brown's class. I would have done that, but I was reminded of the big spectacle she made last year. So I stayed in Mrs. Coleman's class and sucked it up. I left **Sylvanie F. Williams** with mixed feelings about education.

After I figured out there was no Santa or an Easter bunny, I felt stupid. This disappointed me in my elders. Black people follow these holidays out of tradition, but there are implications to following someone else's culture.

I would have appreciated some of those Christmas gifts a lot more had I known my mama was the one buying them. Black people give their power over to the oppressor willingly. We need to stop regurgitating their lies. Black children can handle the truth; there's nothing to fear. The children see this fear then after a while, it's implanted into them. This can lead to unreported mental, physical, or sexual abuse. To children, small things matter; we fail to look at the eroded level of trust. It teaches our children that lying is acceptable. Suppose Europeans choose to celebrate St. Valentine, St. Nicholas, Nimrod, or the Pilgrims; that's their right. These people aren't black, nor do they have anything to do with black culture.

We are so ingrained into European culture, but we know nothing about ours. As I left elementary school, the only thing I learned about us was that we were slaves. We were depicted as docile and affable people **"We Shall Overcome."** Dr. King was a great man, but he appeared weak to a child growing up in the projects. Without proper education of his program, our perceptions become a reality, and in some children, that manifests itself in different ways. It manifested anger in me because I didn't understand why they enslaved us. I saw no reason for the inhumane treatment bestowed upon us. My black Bible shows me black people, while my black church has a white Jesus on the wall. Why is Mrs.Tolley more effective in teaching us than most black teachers at my school? The results of promoting white supremacy would manifest themselves in ways unseen.

My generation was coined "generation x." X is unknown in mathematics, so we were a generation with questions. We were born from the chaos of the **'60s** from those who struggled for civil rights. No one was teaching us about that era. It's disturbing when you consider that some of our parents and grandparents participated. This could have bolstered a sense of pride among us, elevating our self-esteem.

With the entire white hero's on television, church, and school, black people had enough; we didn't need anymore. Whenever I saw African people, they were always dark like me, but black people come in all shades? I asked questions, but I was never given proper answers. I had black male coaches, teachers, and scout leaders, but where were the other black men in my life like my father? I wasn't willing to admit it, but his absence fueled a lot of anger. I did a great job of suppressing it well to the extent that it caused me harm. Like most young black men, everything was run by the matriarchs. Black men should make some decisions about black boys. Most sisters do an outstanding job raising these boys, but only a man can teach manhood. The results of this would manifest themselves in various ways that I will discuss later.

I wondered if my next school would be centered on suppressing the males. Would they bombard us again with heroic tales of white conquest? Could they clear up the confusion of the ethnicity of the people of the Bible? I needed more proof other than my special black Bible.

I relate everything to music, given that my brain records history with soundtracks. **"We Shall Overcome"** was the theme song of that era. As I ventured into junior high, I went in with many questions about myself and my people. I think we should have overcome it by now.

Do you like it? (Yeah!) Do you want it? (Yeah!) Well, if you had it, would you flaunt it? (Hell yeah!) Well, it's yours! "It's Yours" T-La Rock.

CHAPTER 2

THE MESSAGE

"Don't push me cause I'm close to the edge. I'm trying not to lose my head." "The Message" Grandmaster Flash And The Furious Five.

It's the first day of school, and it's like a jungle out there. This was always an unofficial holiday for us. Everyone sported new gear, especially sneakers. It was the same routine every year; first, we checked out the pretty girls, then we caught up on what we did over the summer.

I wound up at **James Derham** because I couldn't get into **Francis W. Gregory.** My mama tried her best to get me in that school. The school board had restrictions on how many children can attend schools in other districts. Gregory was out of my district, so I had to apply for a permit. After I was denied, my mama sent me to James Derham, a few blocks away. I thought junior high school would be different because the teachers were subject-oriented. At first, it was overwhelming to go from class to class and keep up with all the assignments, but I adjusted after a few weeks.

I was really interested in girls. My older brothers had a few girls, and I felt like my time was due. My brother Roosevelt served as an unofficial role model for me. He was a bit older, so I paid attention to how he handled himself. I wanted to be just like him, so I tried to adopt a similar persona. I did some stuff similar to him, like playing sports, joining D.E, and shooting craps, but he and I differ because I was more into the streets.

Around this time, a new form of music made its way into the mainstream. They called it rap. It was developed by young brothers in the streets of New York. These recordings had very catchy beats, and the musicians were more like poets than singers. They all had disc jockeys that did unique things with their records. These DJs had two turntables with a mixer in the middle. They used breaks of records that they extended by going back and forth using the mixer's crossfader. They could mix records to make them sound like new recordings or scratch them. Scratching is moving the record backward and forwards, making sound effects. Scratching was the unique part of these DJs.

The most powerful rap song I had heard around this time was **"The Message" by Grandmaster Flash And The Furious Five. Melle Mel** said, **"Broken glass everywhere. People pissing on the street like they just don't care."** Before the message, no rap song told such a realistic story. Most rap songs during that era were about partying. The next year they followed it up with **"White Lines Don't Do It,"** foretelling a coming drug epidemic.

This wasn't a good time for my family in the back-to-back years. I lost my grandmother and my father. My grandmother was found dead in her home of a stroke, and then my father was murdered. If you saw **"Soul Food,"** this is what my family went through. I learned my grandma was the glue keeping our family together—a rift formed among my mama and my aunts, just like in the movie. Our family gatherings stopped; then, we grew further away from each other. We still saw each other but not as frequently as we did when she was alive.

The murder of my father was troubling; I accompanied my mother when she went to identify his body. His murder affected me in a manner that reverberates today. My fears increased. I don't only have to be aware of white people, but I also had to be aware of some blacks. That one was more frightening because they don't have white skin that makes them easily identifiable. I became selective of my friends. Elders used to preach this, but my father's murder hammered this advice home. I trusted no one, and I was careful of who I was with or where I would go. I felt like an assault had been launched on my whole family. It was determined that my father was killed after a dispute with another brother. The man that killed my father was convicted of his murder; then sent to Angola, where he eventually died. Believe it or not, my father's death gave me a curiosity for the streets. This intrigued me and gave me caution. If I like street life, I can be a pimp like Max Baer in "The Mack," a drug dealer like Sam Scully. I can serve time like my cousin or get killed like my father. I knew I could be a teacher, lawyer, social worker, senator, congressman, or doctor too.

A year earlier, a movie came out that influenced the minds of many youths of my era. The movie was called **"Scarface"** directed by **Brian DePalma,** starring **Al Pacino**. Scarface was about **Tony Montana,** a Cuban refugee who arrived in **Miami** with nothing; then became a major drug lord. This movie was the neighborhood's rave, and everyone enjoyed the violent scenes. The lines of the film have become Shakespearean—disenfranchised black youths connected with Tony Montana. I never saw a movie character so admired or respected.

Meanwhile, the school was a joke; it had become rudimentary. The teachers wrote much stuff on the blackboard that they required us to write down and memorize. Most of them read a few pages in the textbook, asked a few questions then gave us a test at the end of the week. They never delved extensively into any of the subjects they taught us. When I left elementary, I was taught that Christopher Columbus discovered this country, although the Native American Indians were here already. Now I'm in junior high, and they are teaching me about another powerful white man named Alexander. They revere him so much that they proclaim him to be "the great." They go into great detail to teach us of all his great conquest.

They considered the Romans so important that we spent hours praising their accomplishments. The Greeks are treated as the most intelligent people in the world. They spoke of Egypt as if it wasn't even a part of Africa. When Africans were shown in our textbooks, they were always unflattering images. These images didn't endear black people of North America to our people of ancestry being inundated in western society. Those images were shown on purpose to have that intended effect. How come our textbooks never showed African leaders images in suits or military uniforms like **Hailie Selassie, Patrice Lumumba, Jomo Kenyatta, Nelson Mandela, or Idi Amin**? We had world history without identifying the nationality of the Egyptians? When they were teaching us about Egypt in school, the movie **"Cleopatra"** came on television. The movie starred Elizabeth Taylor and Richard Burton. I was astounded that not a single black person was in the movie. I had to read a few National Geographies the next day to ensure **Egypt** was really in **Africa**. I thought I was the one tripping. I learned something important that day not only can the European enslave us, but they can also erase us from history.

They taught us about dinosaurs and troglodytes. The cave people were white folks; they had long hair, were uncivilized, frail, and dirty. We were taught that every human being evolved from these people who co-existed with these huge creatures. The history books told tales of them clubbing their women in the head dragging them into the caves. In the hood, that meant he assaulted and raped her. This kind of behavior was acceptable among this group of people. The department of education had no problem with teaching us this. Considering Mendel's law, how did the caveman become Black, Latino, or Asian? Where did the dinosaurs come from, and where did they go? Why aren't these creatures mentioned in the Bible? I don't recall Noah having a couple of Tyrannosaurus Rexes aboard. None of this was making any sense.

There was no critical thinking involved; we were only required to remember what was written on the blackboard. Besides math or chemistry, no other subjects were challenging. Some teachers left the classroom, often leaving us unsupervised. This sometimes led to disorderly conduct. It was obvious some of them were there just for the check. Most of them cared little about the community or us. They lack the passion required for this profession.

Teaching should be a profession for people who enjoy working with the young. Those who desire to be teachers need to have discipline, patience, empathy, and compassion. Be qualified by the state and licensed by a board. These should be the requirements of a teacher. Those who are devoid of this skill set should seek another occupation. Teachers should be well paid, considering most of them are more than just educators. Some are accountants, counselors, nurses, babysitters, chefs, and party organizers. It would help if you considered how important the people who are often around your children are.

This new music was steadily gaining our interest. We enjoyed rap artists like **Grandmaster Flash and The Furious Five**, **Whodini**, **The Fat Boys**, **Kurtis Blow**, **T-La Rock,** and **The Treacherous 3**. It intrigued me how these brothers crafted a language dance and an art form that revolved around this music.

This wasn't new among talented black people over a century earlier in **New Orleans, Louisiana.** Jazz was created in the same fashion. In their rare time, slaves would gather in **Congo Square,** an area now called **Louis Armstrong Park**. They would play instruments, displaying their talent. By **1895 Charles "Buddy" Bolden** formed the first jazz ensemble, providing the genre's foundation. Hip Hop used a similar blueprint over a century later. In the beginning, jazz wasn't widely accepted, but everyone wanted a part of it when it showed value.

At no time was rap music rawer. Hits by unknown artists were frequently released like **MC Chill, The Master don Committee, The Ultimate MC's, Mantronix, The Z3 Mc's, Roxanne Shante,** and **UTFO**. We were eager to see how far the movement would go. Critics called rap a fad, but it was gaining momentum every day. Since the day I heard **"Rappers Delight,"** the music has been evolving while gaining popularity. Rap music was on the streets, so it had a natural feel of rebellion. Some of our elders said our generation was destructive, and we contributed nothing. Hip Hop was our answer, and it demonstrated what motivated positive young brothers could do. There were many great rap artists, but most of them didn't galvanize the movement. **Kurtis Blow** was an OG to us. We liked **Grandmaster Flash and the Furious Five,** but they dressed like the cats our parents listen to. A new group arrived on the scene from **Hollis Queens, NY,** named **Run-DMC.** The group consisted of **Joseph "Run" Simmons**, **Darryl "DMC" McDaniels,** and **DJ Jason "Jam Master J" Mizell.** We had a strong connection to this group in the sense that their brash unapologetic attitude blended with our sense of rebellion.

"Now we crash through walls, cut through floors, bust through ceilings and knockdown doors." "King Of Rock" Run-DMC.

Run-Dmc wasn't a political rap group, but the hardcore rhymes made up for it. Jam Master Jay's masculine persona, style, and conduct embolden us. Run DMC's contributions would lay the foundation for a conscious group of rap artists to come. Strangely, we shared in the success. When the video for **"King Of Rock"** premiered on MTV, we felt Hip Hop had arrived. They were the first rap group to galvanize the movement.

Like one raised in the projects, I had my share of fights. Fortunately, none of my conflicts ever caused any horrendous acts of violence. Many of these conflicts were based on respect or the need to release testosterone. The next day we would be playing with the same kid we were fighting with the day before. Usually, someone would coerce us to get together; then, we would agree to squash the beef. We were young, but we knew the value of conflict resolution.

In my 8th-grade year, my English teacher Mrs. Tolliver required us to read a book. The book she had us read was **George Orwell's "1984."** This book happens to encompass the way I was feeling. **1984** was the last year; it was the year my father was murdered. So I was curious and felt obligated to read it. In this novel, "big brother" keeps surveillance on everyone using a clever system of mind control. I felt like I had a special relation to this book. It's like I can see things going on while everyone else's mind is under control. Everyone probably bought this book just to pass her class. I bet most of them didn't even read it. I thought she was trying to teach us something outside the box. Rumors floated around that she practiced voodoo, which played a role in people's interest. These rumors were never confirmed, but she played it to her advantage. Most of us were afraid to act out in her class, fearing she would cast a spell on us.

LL Cool J's "Radio" was being blasted on every street corner. Earlier that year, he wows us with his cameo performance in **"Krush Groove,"** a movie loosely based on **Def Jam CEO Russell Simmons's** life. Three movies showcased Hip Hop before Krush Groove's **"Wild Style," "Breaking,"** and **"Beat Street,"** but none of them had stars in them like **Run-DMC, LL Cool J, Sheila E, Kurtis Blow,** and **the Fat Boys**. LL Cool J was the prototype MC; he fit the classic b-boy mold. He wore Fila velour's pumas and a signature Kangol hat. He was a hardcore MC with a lot of range. He displayed his range when he recorded **"I Need Love,"** one of rap's first love ballads. This song showed a different side of LL, establishing him as a sex symbol.

1985 was significant as that year was the year crack had reached New Orleans. Crack is a lethal form of cocaine that the user smokes. It gives an intense high similar to freebasing. It's cheaper than powdered cocaine and can be easily made by combining cocaine with baking soda. The unfortunate effects of crack addiction were starting to show in the community. Some children started coming to school looking neglected. Some of them who used to come to school in the latest fashions now came in cheaper designs or hand-me-downs. Suddenly people who were overweight lost a lot of pounds. The drug game peaked the rise in crime. It became common to hear gunfire every night. The battle over drug turf was a war, and casualties were high. **Charity**, **Flint Goodridge,** and **Methodist** were like military triage stations. Nancy Reagan launched a **"just say no"** anti-drug program. President Reagan declared a **"war on drugs"** in a public address to the nation. The tone was set: we were gonna rid our country of illegal drugs. Most of us didn't know that the so-called "war on drugs" was a war on the Black community. Most states adopted some form of the **Rockefeller drug laws**. Because of these segregated laws, many young men were imprisoned. Most of them were given mandatory minimum sentences for small amounts of crack cocaine, heroin, or marijuana. With no jobs available or skills, young brothers were lured into the drug trade. Misguided young brothers were trying to be like Tony Montana.

Most of the murders went unsolved while their assailants were repeatedly arrested then released. New Orleans had a policy on murder cases called the **"60-day rule**." This policy stated that if no witnesses came forward or they couldn't find sufficient evidence in 60 days, a suspected murderer must be released. This started a cycle of violent offenders released back into the community. This policy would have New Orleans crowned the murder capital of the United States.

Five years prior, we were stunned to hear about a serial killer in **Atlanta, Georgia**. Young black men were coming up dead, and the authorities could not find the killer. The community was complaining of the lackadaisical response by law enforcement. Young black men coming up missing didn't matter to them. This disturbed black people nationwide as rumors ran that the killer was coming to other cities. The whole thing gave me a reason to believe these unknown forces really existed, and these dead brothers in Atlanta prove it. A short time later, the police arrested Wayne Williams and then charged him with just two murders. Wayne Williams was a young, articulate, well mannered young brother. He certainly didn't fit the profile of a man that would do something like this. Williams was found guilty then sentenced to two life terms. I was disappointed that a black man was responsible for these crimes. It's been debated if Wayne Williams was responsible for any of these murders. The conclusion I came to was some blacks can be just as violent as the slave master. With all that I have seen or read about Slavery and Jim Crow, I thought we would be more protective of each other. The whole thing took me months to process.

In the community, we always talked about disingenuous black people. We referred to them as **Uncle Toms**, **House Niggas**, **Sambos**, or **Coons**. An "Uncle Toms" or a "House Niggas" were slaves deemed loyal to the slave master. They worked as agents for the slave master, providing him with information against them. The term originates from the main character in the book "Uncle Tom's Cabin." However, Uncle Tom's characteristics in the novel differ from the ones ascribed to the black community. When black people talk about Uncle Tom, it's usually with great disdain. I used to share in that hatred until I realized an "Uncle Tom" was in no better position than any other slave. I heard the House Negro and Field Negro story detailing how the two differ. After analyzing the two, I concluded that besides one slave working in the field and the other working in the house, there wasn't a difference. The house slave did share certain privileges, but they came at a price. It's widely assumed that the field slave bore much of the slave master's angst.

In most cases, this was true because the Field Negro was more valuable. They cultivated and harvested Massa's crops. When he had a deadline or was agitated, of course, the field slaves would feel the whip; however, I find it impossible that the house slave was treated so well. The house slave, by default, was the most convenient target of Massa. He or she was the first one to feel his or her wrath. We can assume the house slave was the first to be raped, beaten, castrated, or demeaned. The house slave certainly was the most affected psychologically. He or she would internalize the plight of the wicked slave master. How can anyone in their right mind sympathize with such a disgusting individual? A person would have to be mentally ill to feel sad, happy, angry, or depressed based on someone else's feelings. Who would risk their lives to protect such a heinous individual? Many of us failed to recognize that the Field Negro and the House Negro were slaves controlled by the same master.

Of course, the slave master would rely on information from the slaves closer to him. It shouldn't come as a surprise that the slave master could manipulate the house slave; he practically was manipulating them all. It's not like slaves turned in applications to work in the house; then we're specifically selected. We fail to see the value of the House Negro; he or she can be used as a double agent. Most House Negros had the privilege of conversations in the big house. Some of these slaves provided valuable intelligence in many slave revolts. The common denominator was the slave master, who, instead of him being hated, the slaves, in turn, hated each other. This played right into the hands of the slave master, who used this division as a means of control. This has manifested itself in many ways since slavery; for instance, speaking proper English or even attending college can label you a Tom.

I heard two significant records back then. One was named **"PSK"** by **Schoolly D.** He was from **Philadelphia**. I had never heard a rapper from Philly, so I was curious. Come to find out, PSK meant **"Park Side Killers,"** a street gang in Philly that he was alleged to be a member of. This Cat had a different flow; his subject matter was more of the street. I heard rappers talk about the streets but not like this. Rap music was still mostly about partying, but where I was from, many parties didn't start or end well. This was a historical recording for becoming known as **"gangster rap.**"

A short time later, this other record came out; its name was **"6 N The Morning."** This song was by some cat named **Ice-T** out of **South Central**

Los Angeles. The Ice changes the landscape of this new style of rap, bringing it to another level.

Ice-T wasn't new to us; he appeared in the movie **"Breaking"** he also released some hot 12 inches like **"Reckless," "Ya Don't Quit,"** and **"Dog'n The Wax."** **"6 N The Morning"** was on the b side of "Dog'n The Wax." It was a vivid tale of a day in the life of a west coast "G." He takes us on an incredible journey through the hood of South Central, Los Angeles. After hearing his song, I realized that we all go through the same shit. These stories were no different from some of the gangsters I knew. Ice T and Schoolly D sounded like they lived this life. Its **1986** rap music just got real. After hearing these songs, I felt different in a strange way, and I felt empowered.

Since the days when slaves came out to Congo, Square music has always been spiritual to our people. The same spirituality that the slaves used to create Jazz the Gods transferred to the founding fathers of Hip Hop.

They taught us how Christopher Columbus discovered the "new world," but he was greeted by the Native American Indians when he came here. This is another example of how Europeans attempt to erase other people from history. The Europeans only recognize their achievements even if they aren't factual. The nerve of them teaching us the Indians was here first, then giving all the credit to Columbus. The arrogance of this group of people is despicable. I wondered how the Indians allowed the European to conquer them so easily. The Native American Indians were characterized as courageous warriors who were intelligent, brave, and resourceful. Not to mention they knew the land better and outnumbered them. Still, like the European do to the Africans, their history books failed to mention courageous Indian Chiefs like **Geronimo, Sitting Bull, Black Hawk, Cochise,** and **Crazy Horse**. They don't mention Indian tribes like the **Tuscaloosa** or **Seminoles** either. We were misled into thinking that Columbus and his cronies had an easy time conquering them. It wasn't so easy, and it came at a tremendous price. What I didn't know was how far the European would go to reach their objectives. The Europeans have always been at war; they find it impossible to live in peace, not even among themselves. This is why they always had superior weapons. Columbus and his co-defendants had boatloads of ammunition and chemical weapons cloaked in gifts they gave the Indians. These gifts were deliberately infected with smallpox and the flu. When the war's ended, they then used shady treaties to steal land away from the Indians. This reminded me of stories the elders told about white musicians like Elvis. They said he would rip off black musicians and capitalize on their intellectual property. When **Public Enemy** dissed him on **"Fight The Power,"** I understood why.

I studied **Ellis Island,** which is the port that most Europeans came into the United States from. Europeans voluntarily came here from **Germany**, **Ireland**, **France**, **Great Britain,** and **Italy**. The area in which most of them gathered was called the **"Five Points"** in lower **Manhattan, NY**. This area was a hub for poverty, infant mortality, and diseases, and it was notorious for crime. The first organized gangs were established there. This area boasted the highest murder rate in the world. Five Points was a ghetto of epic proportions, but my history books never mention it. They taught us that Columbus discovered America bringing law-abiding Christian white folks.

Every group of people on this planet has been negatively affected by racism white supremacy. Every place the Europeans have appeared, they brought death, destruction, war, famine, upheaval, discomfort, lies, and distrust. They started teaching us about Greek mythology. We spent hours in the classroom discussing these false gods and goddesses. Our teachers spoke of these imaginary people as if they existed. What value did Zeus, Hercules, Aphrodite, Apollo, and Hermes have on our lives? They were another example of supposedly intelligent Europeans. We learned nothing about Africa except that slaves came from there. The Egypt they taught us about was nothing more than a collection of lies and half-truths. The artifacts they allegedly found had European features. The French military leader,

Napoleon Bonaparte, blasted the noses of the Sphinx. He did this out of jealousy of their African features.

My 9th-grade year started with minimal expectations. I had lost interest in school, especially history. Around then, another mini-series came on television named **"Shaka Zulu."** Shaka Zulu was about a great warrior and military genius who becomes king of the Zulu tribe. The mini-series was poorly promoted. I found out about it through word of mouth. The network didn't promote Shaka Zulu as well as they did Roots. I was glued to the television watching this great African king and his beautiful queen portrayed by **Grace Jones**. It was good to see African warriors, military commanders, diplomats, and politicians. After it aired, I expected everyone would be talking about it, but not many people mentioned it. I was perplexed, considering we had a social and pleasure club named after the tribe. A few years ago, when "Roots" came on, people couldn't stop talking about it. It seemed like nobody cared about Shaka Zulu.

In **1969** a brother named **Sam Greenlee** wrote a book called **"The Spook Who Sat By The Door."** The book became a screenplay for a movie of the same title, released in **1973**. Ivan Dixon, starring Lawrence Cook, directed the film. Greenlee's fictional story is about **Dan Freeman,** who becomes the first black CIA agent. The government recruits Freeman and a few other black men to find a token black man for the agency. Freeman excels among the group, eventually becoming a member of the agency. The CIA doesn't know that Freeman cleverly disguised his intentions for joining. He eventually resigns from the agency and then returns to his old neighborhood in Chicago. After he's settled in, Freemen begin to recruit freedom fighters. He starts to train them using the skills he acquired from the CIA. The Spook Who Sat By The Door was short-lived in theaters. Under tremendous pressure from the FBI, the film was pulled from circulation. It was sequestered until 2004 when it was made available on DVD. I found this interesting especially considering all the drug dealers, pimps, drug addicts, and hoes they had us portray. I guess a brother CIA agent who turns out to be a revolutionary didn't meet government approval. I learned what happened to Shaka Zulu wasn't out of the ordinary; actually, I'm surprised they even aired it.

"It's like a jungle sometimes, that makes me wonder how I keep from going under." "The Message" Grandmaster Flash And The Furious Five.

CHAPTER 3

HEY YOUNG WORLD.

"This rap here may cause concern. It's broad and deep. Why don't you listen and learn? Love means happiness that once was strong but due to society even that's turned wrong." "Hey Young World" Slick Rick.

Hey, Young World, it's **86' Run-DMC** got the game on lock. It's my last year at Derham, and I can't wait to get out of here. As my days became numbered, I started to feel like an inmate waiting on my release date. I felt like **Preach** in **"Cooley High"** constantly hiding the fact that I was intelligent. The drug problem was recognizable; many people were addicted to crack, the hood was falling apart. Multitudes of brothers were being locked up or killed. People in the community had become edgy; everyone wasn't as cordial as they used to be. Some crack addicts committed robberies to support their addiction, so the emphasis was placed on security. My mama purchased a nice .38 revolver. I wasn't a stranger to firearms; about a year ago, my cousin gave me a .25. I didn't even have to ask him for it. I think he detected how stressed I used to be sometimes. I know he was tired of my refusal to go places with him because he wanted to hang out in some rough areas. I've heard how powerful guns can make someone feel, but I didn't understand it until I got one. My gun was my passport, enabling me to go anywhere. Except for my cousin, nobody knew I carried it.

I got around a lot, and I finally met some like-minded people. I discussed what school was like with people all over town. I even spoke to a few people who lost a loved one to violence. I met a lot of great people that summer. That's when I started to see the Calliope for what it really was. This made me determined to get out of there. My daddy fought in Vietnam and survived but could not survive in the Calliope projects. The hood was unsafe, and it became a battlefield for opposing drug crews. They were competing to fill the void left after the murder of the kingpin Sam Scully. Crack opened the drug game to all types of immoral behavior. These brazen acts were foreign even to those who had been in the game for years. This new drug stripped people of their morals, so nothing an addict or a dealer wouldn't do.

HANO (Housing Authority Of New Orleans) discontinued most of the maintenance. They used to keep the grounds maintained and conducted routine inspections of tenants. Had these inspections continued, much child neglect could have been uncovered. Many children were left home alone to fend for themselves.

Unbeknownst to my teachers or my mother, I really started disliking school. I never showed it because I wanted to do my best in anything. Most people couldn't tell because I showed a genuine interest in school, and I got good grades. I didn't want to be a distraction, so I kept these feelings to myself. When my mamma or any of my teachers read this, they will be shocked. I wasn't so stupid to dislike school as to hinder myself. If education offered me the best chance at some point, I would continue. This was now on a year-to year basis.

Rap music became major; the release of **Run-Dmc** platinum-selling LP **"Raising Hell"** was proof. The album had a mega-hit single on it named **"Walk This Way"** featuring **Aerosmith**. This song catapulted their careers and reinvigorated Aerosmith's. Rap was crossing over, but no one realized it until **"My Adidas"** was released. That song was magnificent. It made me go out and buy a pair. Imagine how much money Adidas made. They sold tons of sneakers from that song's popularity, but the community never saw a dime. I doubt Run-DMC ever saw their fair share either. This started the commercialization of Hip Hop.

In **1985 Michael Jordan** premiered his new Nike sneaker called the **"Air Jordan."** Besides **Mike Tyson,** Jordan was one of the most influential athletes in the Hip Hop community. People rushed to the stores then stood in line for hours to buy those overpriced sneakers, a trend that continues. Confrontations are known to ensue behind places in line. Some people have been robbed, beaten, and killed over those sneakers. This is why I understood when **Chuck D** said, **"I like Nike but wait a minute the neighborhood supports them put some money in it."** **"Shut Em Down"** **Public Enemy**.

While listening to the radio, I heard a song that would confirm that rap was crossing over. The song was called **"Hold It Now, Hit It"** by **The Beastie Boys**. The Beastie Boys consisted of **Mike D, Ad-Rock,** and **MCA,** three white dudes from **Brooklyn**. Their multi-platinum debut album **"License To Ill"** was released on **Def Jam Records**. I used to listen to **Wail-105** because they always played the hot shit, and I always had a tape in the deck ready to record. We didn't have a lot of money to buy music, so it wasn't uncommon to tape the radio songs. As I listened to this song, I was like, "these dudes sound white." A Caucasian rapper was unheard of, so I quickly dismissed that assertion. New Orleans was one of the stops for the **"Raising Hell"** tour. Run-DMC headlined the tour. Also on tour with them were **LL Cool J, Whodini,** and **The Beastie Boys**. The mystery of their ethnicity would soon be solved.

Whodini was a great rap group out of **Brooklyn** consisting of **Jalil, Ecstasy, and DJ Grandmaster Dee.** Whodini was very polished; their professionalism reminded us of groups like the O' jays or The Main Ingredients. Their music told real-life stories. They endeared us with songs like **"Friends,"**

"One Love," "Funky Beat," and **"The Freaks Come Out At Night."**
They are credited as one of the first rap groups to feature dancers and among
the first to go platinum.

I won tickets for this show off the radio although I was willing to pay. I was
fortunate to be the 9th caller one night on **FM-98**. That saved my brother
and me a few dollars. That evening when we walked into the **Municipal
Auditorium,** we were expecting a great show. Every group on the bill was
hot, so expectations were high. A lot of people had an interest in the Beastie
Boys. I didn't think they were white. I thought the Beastie Boys were some
brothers who were nerds like Steve Urkel or Carlton Banks. Before the tour,
there were no pictures or videos released of them. When the show started,
some white boys dressed like punk rockers came out yelling, **"Let it flow
let yourself go, slow and low that is the tempo." "Slow And Low" The
Beastie Boys**.

Shock overcame the crowd once we realized, "Oh shit, they really are white."
This was a historical moment for race relations. I saw rap shows before this
one and plenty since, but this concert remains one of the best.

Hip Hop had no boundaries. Afrika Bambaataa's Planet Rock explained
it well "rock, rock to the planet rock we don't stop." Afrika Bambaataa is
an important figure in Hip Hop. He started his career in the early 1970's
Djing block parties in the south Bronx. He was a former member of the
Black Spades, a street gang in New York. He created **The Zulu Nation,**
a collection of socially and politically conscious people in Hip Hop. In
1986 he released **"Planet Rock The Album."** It was mostly a collection
of previously released singles like **"Planet Rock"** (1986), **"Looking For
The Perfect Beat"** (1983), and **"Renegades Of Funk"** (1983). Bambaataa
is credited with coining the term Hip Hop and defining all the moving
elements. The elements are defined as graffiti artists, DJs, Break Dancers,
and MCs.

With the emergence of **The Two Live Crew** and **Too Short,** rappers started rapping about sex. This made most of our parents uncomfortable. Too Short was a smooth MC from Oakland. By the time we heard of him, he had already become a local legend and released a few full-length albums. His first nationally released album was **"Born To Mack."** He had a very raunchy unique style of rap.

Luther Campbell was an ambitious young brother out of **Miami, Florida.** He was the CEO of **Luke Sky Walker's** records. He renamed the label **Luke records** after George Lucas sued him for copyright infringement. An early pioneer of southern Hip Hop, the **Two Live Crew** music was danceable, humorous, and raunchy. The group consisted of **Fresh Kid Ice**, **Brother Marquise, Luke,** and **DJ Mr. Mixx**. They were often targets of politicians, law enforcement, or clergy members. Uncle Luke's fight for freedom of speech was significant; it included a case that made it to the Supreme Court. He won his case, proving that you can be vindicated if you are within your rights.

We teenagers suddenly listen to songs like **"Freaky Tales," "Throw That D,"** and **"We Want Some Pussy."** Then at the perfect time, **Kool Moe Dee** comes with **"Go See The Doctor."** Kool Moe Dee was a former member of the **Treacherous Three,** recording as a solo artist. The Treacherous three were considered old school. A younger crop of MCs was replacing pioneer groups like **The Cold Crush Brothers, Grandmaster Flash, and The Furious Five, The Funky Four Plus One,** and even **Kurtis Blow.** Moe Dee was one of the few from that era that stayed relevant. This song was monumental. No MC ever released a song about getting sexually transmitted diseases. The song was informative and well before its time. It pre-dated the AIDS epidemic that was to come. This was a good lesson on what can happen if you have unprotected sex. I don't think anyone of us would have paid attention to his message had it not been articulated so well.

No one was teaching the sons and daughters of the civil rights movement much of anything. The ones that may have taught us something were either dead or locked up. Drugs made our people docile; the leadership we needed was coming through our music. Hip Hop was our religion; the DJs and MCs were the Gods. **Chuck D** referred to rap music as black people's CNN because it contained all the information we needed.

I just about had it with school until **Mr. Player,** my civics teacher, did something powerful. He gave one of the most important assignments I ever had in school. He placed the names of **100** famous black people on the board. The assignment was to turn in typewritten reports on each one of them. He had people up there like **Malcolm X, Booker T. Washington, Fannie Lou Hamer, Thurgood Marshall, Carter G Woodson, George Washington Carver, Toussaint L'Ouverture,** and **Jean Baptiste Point Du Sable.** I was excited to learn about brothers like **Charles Drew, Dr. Daniel Hale Williams, Garrett Morgan, Benjamin Banneker,** and **Adam Clayton Powell.** Besides Carter G. Woodson and Booker T. Washington, I had never heard of most of them. The only thing I really knew about the two was that we had schools named after them. That's when I discovered how powerful Malcolm X was. This man was a giant in the annals of black history. He was uncompromising, courageous, disciplined, and very intelligent. I wonder why his name wasn't ever mentioned around the community. We got a healthy dosage of Martin Luther King with no understanding of his program. I spent the whole week at the public library. I almost didn't finish on time because I got caught up in their extraordinary lives. Some of them were a part of interesting organizations like the **NOI, SNCC, CORE,** and **SCLC.**

This history lesson saved me from dropping out of school that year, but I started to dislike some of my teachers. I never showed it, but I harbored some bad feelings towards them. How is it that Mr. Player can teach us black history while they only teach us of the European? Mr. Player was a civics teacher; he didn't even teach history. My theory was that there was a policy against teaching black history, but Mr. Player dispelled that. That lesson instilled a lot of self-pride in me. I no longer trusted that they would teach me what I needed to know. I decided to ask questions even if it was deemed a distraction.

In my final days at Derham, I was trying to decide what high school I would attend? I love that my mama gave us the option rather than forcing us to attend a school of her choice. She confessed that she did that so we wouldn't have an excuse for not finishing school. I wanted to start this process early to have a good chance of getting into my choice school. I wanted to prepare myself in case I had to apply for a permit. I narrowed my choices to **Kennedy**, **McDonald #35,** and **Fortier**.

Graduating from Derham coincided with my mama's decision to move out of the Calliope. Once she informed me of this decision, I didn't feel as happy as I imagined. I wanted out of the Calliope, but it was all I knew, plus I still had family there. I had gotten a little distant from some of my friends, but at that moment, I realized how much I loved them. They were there for me through some callous times. I knew nowhere I would go would never be the same. I never met such a great group of people again in my life. Home is not just the place where you live; it's also the community. I tried to spend a lot of time with my friends before moving. I knew I would miss **Perry, Marlon, Randy, Charles, Chris, Issac, Kentrell, Corey, Terrence,** and **Tyrone**. I got my first real job at the A&P supermarket. Working kept my mind off from the move. I guess making money can have that effect. Can you believe I had to get a permit for this job? I needed to get permission from the government to make money. Asking permission to do everything was getting on my damn nerves.

After a lot of consideration, I decided to attend **Fortier**. Everyone thought I would attend **Booker T. Washington**. This was based on the fact that many of my family went there, including my older brother. Most of my friends from the Calliope was going there. They all thought we would be able to see each other as usual. Booker T. Washington is located on the outskirts of the Calliope. I felt like if I attended Booker T, it would defeat my mama's purpose of moving us out of the projects. I knew this decision would not be welcomed, so I delayed it as much as possible. I think my mama thought I would go to Booker T or McDonough #35. She never imagined I would attend Fortier, a rival of both schools.

I know some of you are reading this, wondering why this is such a big deal? In New Orleans, the only school that matters to us is your high school. We don't really care what college, trade, or vocational school you attended. The high school you attend is akin to your personality. This may sound strange to some people but not to anyone from New Orleans.

The day after I graduated from Derham, my mama asked me what school I wanted to attend. At the time, I told her I was undecided even though I knew I wanted to go to Fortier. I had started hanging out in **Holly Grove,** a neighborhood about 15 minutes away from the **Calliope**. There were a few homeowners in this neighborhood, and some even owned businesses. The brothers over there seem to have a better understanding of the culture. Most of them were actively involved in the movement. In Holly Grove, I was often in ciphers with Mc's, DJs, b-boys, and graffiti artists. Most of them attended Fortier, the school I plan to enroll in.

I love watching marching bands, especially during the Mardi Gras season. The marching band of **Alcee Fortier, St. Augustine, John F. Kennedy, McDonald 35, Booker T Washington, Cohen, George Washington Carver, John Mc Donald, Xavier Prep,** and **St Mary's** band. Historical black colleges are known for their marching bands' performance and showmanship. Some people attend their football games just to see the bands. Universities like **Southern, Grambling, Jackson State, Florida A & M, Bethune Cookman, Talladega,** and **Alabama State** inspire many aspiring young black musicians. In New Orleans, marching bands are an important part of our culture. Band directors work diligently with young musicians perfecting their sound and marching routines. Fortier's band always sounded great, thanks to the hard work and dedication of **Mr. Elijah Brimmer**. I loved how happy their students, alumni, and faculty looked when they followed that band. I must admit this played a role in my decision to go there.

After a while, my mama got annoyed with my indecision. It was a little more than a month before school started. She decided that we would go down to the school board to get me enrolled the next day. As we drove down there, I informed her of my decision. I can tell she was shocked, especially when she asked me if I said **Fortier**. I said, "Yes, mama, I'm going to the Fo" all she could do was smile. She knew that wherever I went, I would do my best. I knew my brother **Moon** wasn't going to like it either; he attended John McDonald Fortier's fiercest rival. This didn't change how I felt about school, though.

After a while, I started to see crack addicts in Holly Grove. Most of my friends who grew up in Holly Grove knew someone who was addicted to it. Crack was making a negative impact everywhere. How in the hell did it get like this? I discovered in the mid-1980's **Ricky "Freeway" Ross** became one of the biggest drug distributors in the United States. Through the **CIA** plan, he was given access to huge amounts of cocaine and weapons. He set up a successful pipeline for trafficking cocaine based out of Los Angeles using these assets. The CIA connected him with a known Nicaraguan drug lord who became his main supplier. Unknowingly he was used by the CIA to fund a secret war involving the **Nicaraguan Contras**. The whole operation was explained in detail in a **1996 San Jose Mercury** news article written by **Gary Webb**. The US sent money, weapons, and intelligence to Contra's attempt to overthrow the **Sandinista** government. The money to support the terrorist group came from the drugs, they were in fluxing into the black community. Some of this money was used to buy weapons that were exchanged for **American hostages**. The hostages were kidnapped from the American embassy in **Iran** by **Hezbollah,** a radical fundamentalist group supported by **Ayatollah Khomeini**.

After all, this was discovered; **Lieutenant Colonel Oliver North** was summoned before Congress. They asked him to explain why the U.S. Government sold arms to Iran to have American hostages released? This act went counter to the US stance against negotiating with terrorists. They grilled him with questions about the U.S. involvement in supplying money, arms, and intelligence to the Contra's. I don't recall Congress asking him about the CIA involvement in placing drugs and weapons in the black community. In the middle of President Reagan's so-called "war on drugs," all of this was happening right under his nose? Reagan denied knowing anything about the operation, although I find that hard to believe. What sick government would do such a thing? Maybe my conspiracy theories aren't of the base?

I became aware of secret experiments conducted in **Tuskegee, Alabama**. The government allowed scientists to give a large group of black men syphilis deliberately. These men were used as test subjects to see the disease's debilitating effects. This reminded me of how they deliberately gave smallpox infested blankets to Native American Indians. The Europeans have no limits to the harm they would inflict on others.

Was Rick Ross made aware of the plans of involving himself and a foreign terrorist group? Was he ever informed by the CIA that they involved him in their unconstitutional plan? What he did negatively impacted our communities. What were opportunities available to Freeway Rick before he became a successful drug lord?

People talk about how much opportunity is available in the United States around the world. However, this may be true; those opportunities are limited when racism white supremacy factor in. Racism white supremacy is a major component of the United States. This country has benefited from racism white supremacy; it's the ugly truth that America doesn't like to confront. White people and some misinformed blacks believe we are in a "post-racial society." Most of their privileged attitudes have blinded them to racism. They use every excuse to fault those of their discontent, mastering the art of victim-blaming. With all the obvious racism blacks endure world-wide, amazingly, nobody is considered anti-black. It's like every ethnicity has agreed that it's ok to discriminate against black people. Racism is a cause of mental illness, a big problem in our community.

The stress of being black in America takes a toll on us psychologically. A lot of behavior is deemed acceptable to blacks but being labeled crazy isn't. This is an uncomfortable topic that most black people care not to discuss. We are descendants of a group of people stripped of our culture. The loss of our identity still affects us. These issues were never addressed, so they became hereditary. Imagine having to deal with witnessing your brother, sister, mother, or father tortured, killed, or raped. Think about slave moth-ers having their children ripped from their arms, never to be seen again. At no time in America have we not been subjected to racism white supremacy. Our plight is unique, unlike any group of people on this planet. When we stand up to racism white supremacy, some dare to label us as reverse racist, anti-semitic, thugs, radical, unpatriotic, insane, or militant. Many of us don't fight against racism white supremacy because of fear of being given those labels.

We need help from mental health professionals the most, considering the atrocities we are faced with daily. We worry about police brutality, crime, violence, drugs, and poverty every day. Our communities lack the resources to address mental illness. Many states have stripped the community of these resources. Look around the nation; the effects are starting to show. It's con-ceivable every black person in America suffers from some type of mental disorder. They have gone untreated for too long. When a person is hurting, they will seek relief rather than physical or mental. Unfortunately, some of us started self-medicating using alcohol, prescription medication, and illegal drugs. This caused many mentally ill patients to be killed or imprisoned by policemen. Our mental illness approach is ignorant, especially with all the information available.

We need to change our attitude about mental illness then seek professional help. I saw a study that was conducted. Someone placed a black doll and a white doll on a table. They asked a group of black children which doll was ugly, mean, or bad? They all chose the black doll, so when asked which doll was good, pretty, or nice, they all chose the white doll. This is proof that self hatred manifested itself in us early and continues throughout adulthood. This is a form of mental illness. Mental health professionals should reach out to the black community and build a relationship that could lead to progress.

Finally, the moving day arrived. It was an emotional day for my family; my mama seemed agitated the whole time. It may have been the projects, but it was all we ever knew. It took us a few trips, but we finally got everything out of the house. I found out that day that moving is a lot of work. On our last trip, I sat on the back of the truck, looking at the **CP3** until it was no longer visible. I understand how rappers can confess their love for their hood. Like anyone, we all cherish the places of our origin. I'm going to miss **Rosenwald Park, Mr. Dan's, Mrs. Lou's, Bus Stop Po Boys, Jumping Jimmy's,** and **Split Seconds**. There will never be anything like **Mrs. Mary's** popcorn balls or some hot gossip coming out of **Rose Tavern**.

We moved to a good neighborhood. The house was a great shotgun with a nice backyard. I already knew a few people that lived around there. One of them was my man Brian Vaughn. Brian was a great breakdancer, he and I attended Derham. He introduced me to his older brother Charlie who everyone called **Charlie-V**. Charlie-V was the first legitimate graffiti artist I ever met. His pieces would give Picasso a run for his money. This brother helped to expand my knowledge of Hip Hop culture. He humbly shared a lot of information on the culture with me daily. He had tapes from DJs I never heard of, like **Red Alert, Chuck Chill Out, Davy Dmx,** and **Mr. Magic**. He possessed a library of magazine articles, graffiti art, tapes, and news clippings. He put me on to artists like **Big Daddy Kane, Public Enemy,** and **Boogie Down Productions,** just to name a few. The good thing is he lived right around the corner.

Around that same time, I met a cat named **Pecky,** aka **DJ Icy Ice.** He was a dope DJ. I credit him for putting me on to artists like **Ice-T, Stetsasonic,** and **The Show Boys**. The Show boy's hit song **"Drag Rap"** would become the foundation of New Orleans base bounce. He made me the first official mixtape I ever got from a DJ. This was a great neighborhood, but sometimes I longed to be back in the Calliope. I returned to hang out for several weeks, but after a while, I stopped. I was devoted to Hip Hop. It was the only thing that mattered to me. I found a great job for a person of my age that paid better than A&P. I was an original member of the TCA **Young Entrepreneurship Program**. YEP was a program where we were provided with a business then taught how to run it all by ourselves. This job taught me valuable business experience. I even got a little television exposure when our story aired on the news. **Total Community Action** was a community-based organization with programs that helped out the community. It felt good working for an organization that did so much good in the community. As YEP manager, this brought me into places I thought I would never go. I met people I thought I would never meet, like CEOs of fortune 500 companies, senators, members of Congress, and city council members. I even met Mayor Sidney Bartholomew. The director of TCA **Mr. Dangerfeld** showed us a lot of love. We used to crack jokes about how much he resembled Fredrick Douglas. Mr. Dangerfeld displayed leadership that Frederick Douglas would have been proud of. He was result orientated, which proved to be valuable.

When I finally stepped foot in Fortier, I was overwhelmed by its size. The school was huge. I was inside Booker T. and John Mac, but Fortier was just as big. Believe it or not, I attended Fortier without ever seeing the building. Fortier was a cool ass school. I thought I made the right decision. I was surprised to find out we had a school newspaper called **"The Tarpon Talk."** I felt honored to become a member of the staff. Composing rap songs fueled my love for writing. The students at Fortier demonstrated a tremendous amount of school pride. When I was at Derham, it felt like nobody cared about that school. Most of our events had limited participation, but here, the students get into it all; it's contagious.

"Righteous laws are overdue and this is a message that the Ruler Rick threw and it's true." "Hey Young World" Slick Rick.

CHAPTER 4

FIGHT THE POWER.

"Education is the passport to the future, for tomorrow belongs to those who prepare for it today." Malcolm X.

Euclid, Aristotle, Democritus, Socrates, Sir Issac Newton, Constantine, and Julius Caesar yep, they teach that bullshit here too, but thanks to Mr. Player. I was aware of us getting played. I was no longer interested in hearing about how great the Europeans are. My tolerance had long ago waned. That summer, I read a couple of books, poems, and a few short stories from authors like **Richard Wright, Walter Mosley, Sonia Sanchez,** and **Maya Angelo.** It was **1987,** I came a long way, but like Hip Hop, I still had a long way to go. I wanted more out of education and a better understanding of things in the world. I needed answers to these questions that troubled me since I was young. I started to see things culminate in life and Hip Hop almost simultaneously.

When I left school, a dispute took place on the Freret bus between the bus driver and some brother who boarded the bus. The caucasian driver called the police because they got on the bus at the next stop. After talking with the bus driver for a few minutes, the two white officers proceeded towards the back of the bus. When they got there, they started questioning the wrong brother. The brother they were questioning was with his girl; they got on the bus at the same time I did. Next thing you know, the police are whipping his ass. The sister jumped up to defend him then the other policeman punched her in the face. They both were handcuffed then quickly removed from the bus. If we had cell phones back then, someone would have recorded the whole thing. This was significant because I heard about police misconduct, but I had never witnessed it. The whole thing happened so fast it gave everyone little time to react. I couldn't believe what I witnessed that day. I'm embarrassed to say the incident left me a little shook. Feeling that way annoyed the shit out of me too.

It made me think about something that occurred seven years earlier. I was too young to understand what was going on then, so I went to the library to research the incidents. On the night of **November 9, 1980, NOPD** officer **Gregory Neupert** was killed near the **Fisher** housing projects. The Fisher was located in **Algiers**, a town on the west bank of New Orleans. In desperation to solve his murder, overzealous police officers proceeded to harass, falsely arrest and brutalize people in the community. These illegal raids culminated in the violent murders of four innocent people **James Billy**, **Reginald Miles**, **Raymond Ferdinand,** and **Sherry Singleton**. It was reported that Ms. Singleton was killed in the bathtub in front of her four-year-old son. Despite Orris Buckner's testimony, the only black officer involved, only three of the seven officers involved were convicted. They each received only five years in prison for their roles in civil rights violations, but none of the officers was charged for the murders. Some community people testified that officer Neupert was killed by two white men while conducting a drug transaction.

The elders used to tell us stories about the confrontations the Black Panthers had with the police. I embraced their revolutionary spirit; there's much to be admired about them. Their bravery and dedication to the community were outstanding. The Panthers tried to develop a program to curtail incidents between members of the black community and law enforcement. I could tell you more, but I will discuss them later.

I started having reservations about attending Fortier. Academically it reminded me of Derham. I chose Fortier over McDonough 35, which was better academically, especially among public schools. Every time those thoughts came to mind, I would be like, **"Fortier cooler than a fan."** Finally, we had a good football team to match that great band. Booker T Washington and McDonough 35 stranglehold on the district was coming to an end. Later that year, we won district, then we made a deep playoff run. **Coach Alfred Levy** did an excellent job motivating young student-athletes. Several of his players received college scholarships; some even played in the NFL.

Hanging with Charlie-V was then a routine. On one occasion, I noticed he had a tape of a group named **Public Enemy**. I saw their album recently in **Odyssey** while buying some 12 inches. I had a mixer and two turntables at home. If I liked an album, I would make a tape of it to play in my walkman. At first, I was turned off because the group was massive similar to the Furious Five. **Run DMC** said, **"The good news is that there is a crew, not five, not four, not three just two."** "Jam Master Jay" Run-DMC. Kool Moe Dee was even solo now besides **Stetsasonic.** I cared not to listen to a bunch of cats rapping. I thought every one of them brothers rapped, including the S1W'S. The industry wasn't the huge promotional machine it is today, so I had no idea who did what in this group. So here's the tape of the album I passed up a few days ago. I had no idea who these brothers were, but this group was about to change my life.

Reluctantly I asked him to play the tape; he was about to rewind it, but I urged him to let it play.

"You go ooh and ahh when I jump in my car. People treat me like Kareem Abdul Jabbar." "Time Bomb" Public Enemy.

This was the first rhyme I heard from one of the most influential rap groups of all time. The next day I purchased the album **"Yo Bum Rush**

The Show." Public Enemy was a black power movement all by itself. They raised the bar for rap artists, out of Long Island, New York. Highly structured P.E. had a minister of information named **Professor Griff**, a hype man named **Flavor Flav,** a DJ named **Terminator X,** and a security unit called the **S1W's. Chuck D,** the hard rhymer, was the perfect frontman for this group. He embodied all our heroes' revolutionary spirit in the black power movement. This was a well put-together group featuring a hype man, a security unit, and a minister of information. This was all new to rap music. Flavor Flav was uncanny and hilarious; he made Chuck D and Professor Griff's tough messages more palatable to the listener. When Professor Griff wasn't leading the security unit, he would drop knowledge on us.

Shortly after that, I heard about another new group named **Eric B and Rakim**. Everyone talked about how good their album was, but when I heard **DJ King Jaz** say it, that did it for me. I knew he didn't spin any wack shit, so I always listen to his advice. That day I was supposed to stop by **Brown Sugar Records** to buy their album, but it slipped my mind. On the way home, I kept hearing this hot beat with a sample of **Dennis Edwards "Don't Look Any Further."** All of the ballers were playing this song out of their whips. When I got home that day, my older brother **Moon** had copped a few tapes. One of them was **"Paid In Full."**

I knew he might be pissed behind me opening up his shit, but I didn't care. Without hesitation, I put it in my tape deck. Then instantly, I became amazed at what I was listening to. I had never heard an MC like him before. **Rakim Allah** was the perfect MC; he was a gifted lyricist with a serious flow. I never heard the English language articulated so brilliantly. His delivery was unlike any MC I ever heard. At the time, most MCs rapped aggressively, but Rakim rapped like he was speaking to you. This made him easy to listen to and better understand. His name was interesting; not many knew what it meant, but we knew it had meaning **("Ra" the sun god "Kim" from the land of Kemet)**. His fans included cats in the streets, college students, women, children, old and new school Hip Hop heads. Rakim remains among the greatest MCs in the history of rap music. In his song **"Move The Crowd"** he said something interesting. **"With knowledge of self, there's no problem I couldn't solve at 360 degrees. I revolve." "Move The Crowd." Eric B And Rakim**. That was the first time I heard someone say that. I felt like he was speaking to me like he felt my inner struggles with history in my all-black school. Nobody was teaching us "knowledge of self."

We were taught the Greeks, Romans, Italians, Irish, and Egyptians that were mysteriously moved out of Africa. They taught us more about the Chinese, Koreans, and the Japanese than they were about Africans.

Rakim declaring he had **"knowledge of self"** inspired me; I thought if he had it, then I could get it too. Without realizing that's what Hip Hop was inspiring me to do. Rakim and Public Enemy taught me how to deal with school. I will learn about Europeans someday; this information may be valuable. When I'm away from school, I will seek out people or information that could teach me what they fail to. Jewels dropped by Rakim in a rap song stopped me from dropping out of school. I never entertained those thoughts ever again.

On another occasion, while I was in Odyssey, I noticed this shocking album cover. The cover had these two brothers on it brandishing guns and shit calling themselves **Boogie Down Productions**. I dismissed them as hooligans trying to ruin Hip Hop. The next day I went to see Charlie-V; as I greeted Brain, he instructed me to the back of the house where he was. As I'm entering his house, I hear this wicked guitar sample with some brother sounding all reggae and shit chanting, **"the p is for free but the crack cost money oh yeah." "P For Free" Boogie Down Productions**.

This song draws you in, and you can tell this guy will tell an interesting story. I was surprised to find out this was the same album I saw the other day. I never heard an MC with so many different styles. BDP was from the

South Bronx. The group consisted of **DJ Scott La Rock, Krs-One,** and **D Nice**; their album **"Criminal Minded"** was genius. They reminded us of the clever OG's we knew from the hood. BDP took what Ice T and Schoolly D were doing to the next level. This was a dope album, but it could be classified as a so-called **"gangster rap"** album. This was the first time I heard an emcee address a beef he had with another rapper on wax.

"What's the matter with your MC, Marley Marl? Don't know you know that he's out of touch? What's the matter with your DJ MC Shan? On the wheels of steel, Marlon sucks." "The Bridge Is Over" Boogie Down Productions.

"It was once said by a man who couldn't quit dope man please can I have another hit?" "Dope Man" NWA. This man sounds hungry, raw, and angry, just like me. The beat sounds aggressive, almost East Coast but gangster. This song took so-called "gangsta rap" to a new stratosphere. **NWA (Niggaz With Attitude)** was the world's most dangerous group. This group scared the shit out of America. The group hailed from **Compton, California** home to some of the most notorious street gangs. The group consisted of **Eazy E, Ice Cube, MC Ren, Doctor Dre,** and **DJ Yella**; Ice Cube tells a vivid story of a west coast "G." For better or worse, NWA messages were accepted. One group member stated that NWA was what the youth would be like if Public Enemy was ever shut down.

Then **"Rhyme Pays"** was released as Ice-T's debut album. The Ice sets the standard for this growing genre of rap. His album was a bit different; he deals with the full spectrum of gangsta life. This includes the consequences, as he demonstrated in **"Pain."** He identifies some of those gang sets we often heard about in Los Angeles.

"The Rolling 60's to the Nickerson G's, The Pueblos, The Grape Streets this is what I see. The Jungle, The 30's, The V.N.G life in L.A. ain't no cup of tea." He addresses excessive force by police officers. **"Cops**

hate kids, kids hate cops, cops kill kids with warning shots. What is a crime and what is not? What is justice I think I forgot?" "Squeeze The Trigger"

These stories were real to us. We dealt with it every day. We didn't have gangs in New Orleans, but we had drug crews which isn't much different.

What fosters the climate for gangs to exist in the first place? We were dealing with an absence of leadership. The leaders we had were really agents of white supremacy; we allowed them to choose these leaders then stood behind their wack choices. Then we allowed them to make demagogues of our true leaders. Although we know they don't have our best interest in mind, we blindly follow the Europeans.

To get a better understanding, let's take a look at integration. What is widely believed to be the start of desegregation was **Brown VS The Board Of Education Of Topeka, Kansas (1954).** In this landmark case, the Supreme Court ruled that states that establish separate schools based on race be unconstitutional. The biggest gain of desegregation would be the **Civil Rights Act (1964)** which ended discrimination based on race, sex, religion, or national origin. Other landmark rulings by the courts would come later, like **The Fair Housing Act (1968),** which outlawed discrimination in housing.

Integration did a great disservice to the black community. If we give it some careful thought, it's not hard to see. Let's examine all those "sit-ins" that we organized. The first one occurred on **February 1, 1960,** when four students from **North Carolina Agricultural and Technical College (Joseph McNeil, Franklin McCain, David Richmond, and Ezell Blair Jr)** sat down at the counter of Woolworth's then asked to be served. Of course, that wasn't going to happen because it was white only they didn't serve blacks. That year alone, it was estimated that over 3,000 college students were arrested in similar demonstrations. In most of these "sit in's" these young people were subjected to a lot of humiliation. They endured condiments being dumped on them, hot water, acid, and they were beaten. I understood the need for social and political change; I just didn't understand the means they went about getting it. At the time, there were black-owned businesses in the community. Many of these business owners lived in the community. Some served as mentors while providing jobs. They understood their customers' needs, forging personal relationships with the community. So why did we feel the need to "sit-in" any business only to be humiliated, beaten, or arrested? Besides, they already had white-owned businesses in the community. What if we had remained loyal to these black-owned businesses? We could have our own black Woolworths, McDonald's, Macy's, Wal-Mart, JCPenney, or Sears. We could be independent economically and not codependent.

Take a look at prosperous black communities like Rosewood in Levy County, Florida, and Black Wall Street in Tulsa, Oklahoma. These towns boasted all black professionals, including doctors, nurses, lawyers, teachers, dentists, and carpenters. They were independent communities, and all the money made there was reciprocated around the town. These towns were destroyed by enraged envious white people over false allegations of rape by white women. In Tulsa, an estimated 3,000 people were killed and 600 businesses destroyed. The riots were encouraged by law enforcement that stood by doing nothing, and some even participated. It would have been impossible to prosecute everyone involved because it was a riot. The government should have intervened by sending in the National Guard to restore order. This could have saved lives and prevented the loss of property. Instead of doing that, the National Guard arrived and started rounding up black people. Some white people flew airplanes over the area dropping firebombs. These are the people we wanted to integrate with. How selfish is the European we can't have businesses of our own without having them destroyed, and we aren't welcomed in theirs? The alleged rapes that started the riots were poorly investigated.

What made a burger at Woolworth's better than one at the businesses in your own community? These business owners appreciate your patronage. Most of them went out of business after integration. Plenty of black people bypassed them, excited that they could now shop among whites. Businesses that traditionally discriminated against us welcome our patronage. Integration was foolish; in the end, Dr. King didn't even endorse it.

In **1955 Emmett Louis Till** was murdered in a town called Money, Mississippi. The young Mr. Till was visiting from Chicago when he allegedly flirted with a white woman named Carolyn Bryant. Offended by his jester, she told her husband, Roy. In outrage, Roy Bryant and John "J.W.," William Milam rode around town searching for Mr. Till. They eventually found him at his uncle Mose Wright's home, where they kidnapped and murdered him. When his kidnapping was reported, a search party was sent out to find the brother. When they finally found him, he had a fan tied around his neck, and his face was disfigured. In his murder trial, Bryant and Milam were found not guilty by an all-white jury. Juries in towns like Money seated members of the white citizen council, making fair trials impossible for blacks.

This brings up an interesting point about American justice. Most black people hate jury duty. Some of us will do anything to duck this civic right. We often complain about the injustices we face in the judicial system but spurn the opportunity to do something about it. Black folks get no juries of our peers because our peers don't want to be on the jury. On **January 24, 1956,** look magazine published an interview conducted with Bryant and Milam. In the paid interview, both men confessed to murdering Mr. Till.

Then I saw **"Mandingo"** this film premiered in **1975** starring former heavyweight champion **Ken Norton**. Norton plays a Mandingo slave named Ganymede, who is a trained fighter. Hammond, his slave master, fights him for money and uses him as a stud. Hammond's life is complicated the night of his wedding after discovering that Blanche wasn't a virgin. She confessed to lying to him about her virginity which her brother broke. This made him feel betrayed and regretting that he married her. He then turns to slave women for affection; he rapes several of them who have and abort a number of his children. While he's away from the plantation on business, Blanche seduces Ganymede, forcing him into an affair. She reconciles with her husband, although she and he never stop their affairs. After a while, she discovers she's pregnant, and they both are excited in anticipation of their first child. She believes the child is Hammonds; however, it turns out to be Ganymedes. She's forced to tell the truth of the affair then is murdered. An enraged Hammond then forces Ganymede into a boiling kettle of water where he's tortured and killed. So white men would burn down towns, boil a man alive or leave black men disfigured to protect the virtue of a white woman. To this day, a white woman crying can invoke a deadly reaction from the white community. The slave owner raped black women at will but had the nerve to be upset when his woman was violated. This is the violence that has happened historically in America. It's the hate that hate made.

As Hip Hop started to rise, here come the powers that be. Rappers like NWA, BDP, and Ice T were connected to the crime. Rap music and violence had become synonymous with the media sensationalizing this. Overtly Hip Hop was being connected to criminals. They pumped up crime statistics then tried to connect them to rap music. Every news cycle started with a murder. They broadcast that other blacks kill 93% of the black people killed in America. They tout these statistics without acknowledging that other whites kill 83% of white people in America. This sends out the narrative that black culture is built upon violence. I do not deny that people get killed in the hood every day. I'm just rejecting the notion that violence is an issue that blacks deal with only. This is historically inaccurate, especially when you consider everyone's violent history.

June 28, **1914,** Austria's Arch Duke Ferdinand's assassination touched off a catastrophic event that changed history. This incident is widely recognized as what started **World War 1**. World War 1 lasted from **June 28, 1914,** to **November 11, 1918**. The people of Europe were tired of the imperialistic foreign policy of superpowers like **Germany**, **Russia**, **Great Britain,** and **France.** Approximately **65 million** troops were deployed, mostly white men except for **Japan.** On **April 6, 1917,** the **United States** became involved in backing its allies **Great Britain.** President Woodrow Wilson was under pressure from the American people who wanted a response to several US ships' sunk by German U Boats. An estimated **37 million** people were killed in this war, predominantly white people killing white people.

September 1, 1939, Poland's invasion by Germany is believed to be the event that started **World War 2**. This war lasted until **September 2, 1945.** The conflict involved **Britain, Russia, Poland, Germany, France, Yugoslavia, Italy, Hungary,** and **Romania**. There were also several non-European countries like **Japan, Brazil, China,** and **The Philippines.** Approximately **100 million troops** were deployed in this war. Approximately **65 million** fatalities resulted again; mostly white people killed each other. The most horrific incident to take place during this time was the murder of approximately **6 million** Jews in what is called the **Holocaust**. Here we have **Adolph Hitler,** a white dictator authorizing the extermination of millions of other innocent white people.

China and **Japan** had been at war since **1931**. This conflict began when China became fed up with Japan's imperialistic policies dating back to the **1800s**. In **1937** this war was engulfed into World War 2 after Japan invaded China. On **December 7, 1941,** Japan bombed **Pearl Harbor,** a naval base in **Hawaii.** After this unprovoked attack on American soil, the **United States** became involved. Scores of Asians were killed, mostly by Europeans or other Asians in this conflict. An estimated **2.5 million** Japanese and approximately **20 million** Chinese were killed. **August 6 -9, 1945,** the

United States dropped atomic bombs over **Hiroshima** and **Nagasaki cities**, killing an estimated **129,000** people, mostly civilians. These are the numbers accounted for at the time of the bombings, not those who died later of radiation poisoning. This was the only time a nuclear weapon was used at war.

The **Korean war** spanned from **1950-1953,** putting the North Koreans against their brothers from the south. The US and Russia manipulated this war; both superpowers supplied troops and arms to each side. During the "cold war," the Korean people were used as pawns. There were an estimated **3 million** casualties which were primarily Koreans killing Koreans.

Latinos were entrenched in the **Mexican revolution,** which eventually turned into the **Spanish Civil War.** This war started in **1910** when a group led by **Francisco Madero** came together to restore the country's constitution. In both of these wars, there were an estimated **1 million** casualties of Latinos killing each other.

The **Iran** and **Iraq war** started **September 22, 1980,** and lasted until **August of 88'.** This war started over a border dispute. Iraq Prime Minister Saddam Hussein was attempting to re-claim Shatt al-Arab, a section of the Persian Gulf that was turned over in a **1975** treaty. There were scores of troops and civilians killed in this war using firearms, explosives, and chemical weapons. Over **1 million** troops and civilians were killed during the eight years.

The Mafia or La Cosa Nostra is a crime syndicate that started in Sicily sometime during the mid 19th century. Most of their members were immigrants who entered the United States through Ellis Island. They came from Northern and Western European countries like **Ireland, England, Germany, Italy,** and **Scandinavia.** They settled in **Five Points** then formulated gangs that eventually became the Mafia. Their crimes were so sophisticated that special law enforcement units were created to curtail them. Through their connections with their **European** counterparts in the **United Kingdom,** they seized control of the opium trade from the Chinese. Then they started importing illegal drugs into the United States. They got rich from these ventures and the selling of alcohol during prohibition. They invented the drive-by; they drove Studebaker's, Lincolns, and Chevy's firing through the windows using Tommy guns with magazine clips. Scores of people were killed, shootings and bombings became commonplace—all of this involved **Italians**, **Jews**, and **Irishmen** killing each other.

The Mexican drug cartels were established in the late **1970s**. These cartels have always been a brutal force throughout **Mexico**, **Central America,** and **South America**. It's been estimated that up to **2 million** or more people have been killed. Keep in mind these figures are from these countries, not from the United States. I won't be hypocritical and not to mention the tribal warfare that's been happening in Africa for decades. African warlords are supplied arms from countries like the United States and Britain. They then declare war on each other like they do in both countries.

Violent crimes happen in every community, but the media makes it look like it only happens in ours. This gives the world the illusion that we are more prone to violence. These examples should dispel that notion. **Public Enemy** warned us, **"Don't Believe The Hype."**

I know some hard-working journalists do their best to present credible stories. They have integrity, and they try to present honest stories. I understand journalists are under pressure as a member of my school newspaper. I learned that. I always found myself up against the deadline. I know professional journalists are under a lot more pressure. I took journalism seriously because I knew that it could be a profession. We released the "Tarpon Talk" weekly. Most of our articles were about our student-athletes, teachers, administrators, events, and students. We had an editorial page that

I eventually started writing. The stress of this job shouldn't be used as an excuse for lazy or disingenuous journalism. This wouldn't be the last time the media attacked Hip Hop; we all knew that. Most of us in the movement took these attacks personally.

Every form of black music was hijacked. For instance, when most people envision rock and roll, they immediately think of **Elvis Presley, Jerry Lee Lewis,** or **Buddy Holly.** Not **Chuck Berry, Louis Jordan, Little Richard, Fats Domino,** or **Ray Charles.** Ask the average person about jazz most of them would mention **Frank Sinatra, Benny Goodman,** or **Dave Brubeck.** Not **Louis Armstrong, Duke Ellington, Charlie Parker,** or **Dizzy Gillespie.** Guitar notes by **Jimi Hendrix** created a rock genre called **psychedelic** and **heavy metal.** We were not going to allow that to happen to rap music. Rap music was all we had. Hollywood ignored black youth. **Eddie Murphy's Beverly Hills Cop** was the only movie that cast a black lead.

The frenzy over rap lyrics worked against the powers that be. All the media attention aroused curiosity, especially among white kids. It awakened a new revolutionary spirituality among black kids, which was the reason behind the negative media campaign. Many of us wondered why they are attacking rap when it's mostly PG? Former vice president **Al Gore's** wife **Tipper** launched a censorship campaign on what she considered offensive rap lyrics. She founded the **PMRC** (Parents Music Resource Center) and **Susan Baker, Pam Howar,** and **Sally Nevius.** She eventually pressured the recording industry into placing warning labels on albums. Mrs. Gore was annoyed by young black people making money. Foolishly some of our elders launched campaigns similar like **Reverend Calvin Butts** and **C. Delores Tucker.** It seemed hypocritical, considering our elders grew up listening to music from the streets.

"I'm your mama, I'm your daddy, I'm that nigga in the alley. I'm your doctor when in need. Want some coke, have some weed. You know me,

I'm your friend. Your main boy, thick and thin. I'm your pusher man."
"Pusher Man." Curtis Mayfield 1972.

Dope Man is a little more graphic, but besides the language the same message is being conveyed. No civil rights organization defended Hip Hop, not the NAACP or the Urban League. Instead of our elders creating meaningful dialogue with us, they launched an attack.

Take a look at **Woodstock,** the music festival held **Aug 15-18, 1969,** in Woodstock, New York—billed as "The Festival Of Peace," an astounding 32 acts performed during the three days. It's estimated that approximately **400,000** people attended, mostly white folks stoned out of their minds. Drug usage was rampant at this festival; you can ask anyone who attended. Most of the drugs were used in the plain open view of law enforcement. The same thing happened two years earlier at the **Monterey Pop Festival**. I bet Mrs. Gore or some of her minions attended one of these festivals. Drugs weren't allowed at the rap shows I had been to. Violent movies like Scarface, The Terminator, and Rambo were released to blockbuster audiences. The actors in these movies were respected for their art, while rap artists were scrutinized.

The parental guidance most of our parents had enjoyed wasn't conveyed. Rap music was providing us with that guidance. Hip Hop was the only thing keeping us sane. It was **1987,** only **19 years** after the death of **Dr. King**. **Twenty four years** since **Malcolm X** was assassinated, what the hell happened to us?

Music plays a role in society. It can tell you the history of an era. The frequency has always determined the state of mind of the people. By the end of the '70s, **James Brown's** reign in the music industry started to decline. He was one of the few artists of our parents' time that my generation could relate to. His song **"Give It Up Turn It Loose"** is the official Hip Hop anthem. Because of his influence, DJs began to sample his recordings, and producers like **Marly Marl** cleverly used his music. Artists like him with socio-political messages weren't around anymore.

Black people were on their way to fully be integrated. The music became danceable and light-hearted with a driving beat. Everyone called this new music **disco**. With this new music came an attitude of freedom. Everyone was expressing it by using drugs, having a lot of sex, and through their intimate relationships. All of the boundaries were broken, and the restrictions were lifted. Some people found comfort in alternative lifestyles. Desegregation created a curiosity among the races. Clubs like **Studio 54** embodied the spirit of life post-integration. White lines of cocaine flowed freely through nostrils. Pills were being popped like corn. Platform shoes adorn many feet—mink coats, polyester suits in wild colors and black-fisted picks. Just let loose forget all that shit that happened a few years ago. Let's all get down and Boogie Oogie Oogie.

The food industry developed all kinds of simple foods, making it easy to prepare meals. Instant potatoes, macaroni, and cheese in a box, broccoli in a bag, and stove top stuffing. These new inventions made cooking dinner easy, saving plenty of time. All you had to do is put the children to bed, hit the club, and dance, dance, dance. Segregation was over, and blacks were free to shop at D.H. Holmes, Krause, Dillards, and the beloved Woolworths.

Disco was making a lot of money, but it wasn't without its critics despite the huge revenue coming in. They claimed that the music lacked creativity; the production was simple, and it promoted a deviant lifestyle. Disco changed the beat, it was a constant catchy rhythm. Most of the top artists, producers, writers, arrangers, and musicians of that era were black. Great artists like **Issac Hayes**, **The O' Jays**, **The Pointer Sisters**, and **Barry White** were overlooked. These exceptional artists were placed in the same category as everyone else. A lot of radio stations were dedicated exclusively to disco. All the other stations had spots for it in their programming. The music industry was bombarded with a plethora of disco songs. Because of the simplicity of the beat, it was easy to replicate. It got to ridiculous levels. The Disco Duck, Sesame Street Disco, Mickey Mouse Disco, and even Ethel Merman recorded a disco album. The backlash was due to come especially among unhappy rock musicians and radio personnel.

It culminated **July 12, 1979,** in **Chicago** at **Comiskey Park,** the home field of the **Chicago White Sox. Steve Dahl,** a popular radio personality, was upset after WDAI, an exclusive disco station, fired him. With the authorization of White Sox's owner Bill Veek, he staged a small protest of his termination. The object of the protest was to blow up a huge crate of disco records during the intermission of the baseball game. The event would have gone as planned, except more people came out than they anticipated. A huge crowd gathered in Comiskey Park. They weren't there for the game. They were there to express their hatred for disco. After the explosion, the mostly white crowd got out of hand, bum-rushing the field. Several injuries resulted in some of them being arrested. In one night what took recording companies a few years to build was destroyed.

This incident went worldwide, and the rippled effects sealed disco's fate. Most of the musicians of that era were blacklisted. Some of their careers never recovered. I place most of the blame on the greedy record companies. They stiffed the creativity of their artist, forcing them to record disco only. Not all of them did it this way; some were savvier. These companies had their artists record a few disco songs that they promoted better than others. With all they knew about the music business, they should have known the beat had to change. This was no different from the big band era having to consent to bebop. **Louis Armstrong** and **Dizzy Gillespie** feuded quite a bit about this. It was going to be difficult to do, but it became necessary. These companies were only interested in profits.

The artist shares some of the responsibility as well. They should have been aware of the same then demanded more creativity. Another point not to be missed is that many white musicians were struggling. Most disco artists were black. Disco association with homosexuality fuels a lot of the hate too.

It's true disco attracted many homosexuals but to hate a whole genre of music just based on that is ignorance. Only a few disco artists were open about their sexuality. Some rock artists' sexuality can be questioned in the same manner. This made me think about something. It was a disco song that helped to bring rap to fruition. Strangely, **Chic** was conveying a message. It's like they were saying if you're not careful, those **"Good Times"** can come to an end.

Rap music was no longer about one song or one group. Out of **Philly** came **Jazzy Jeff and the Fresh Prince**. Their debut album **"Rock The House"** was a commercial success. It maintained the balance that personified the era. We all can see something special in this duo. The Fresh Prince was charismatic and charming. **Jazzy Jeff** was a turntable technician. He and other DJs from Philly like **Cash Money**, **DJ Miz,** and **Tat Money** established Philadelphia as a major hub for great DJs. **LL Cool J** released **"Bigger And Deffer,"** a great sophomore album building him to be the Hip Hop icon he was to become. **MC Shan** released **"Down By Law."** Coming out of **Queens Bridge,** MC Shan and legendary producer **Marly Marl** record a dope album. From **Mount Vernon** came **Heavy D and The Boyz**. They dropped their debut album **"Living Large**." We were not going to quit; we were determined to **"Make everyone see you got to fight the powers that be"** **"Fight The Power"** Public Enemy.

CHAPTER 5

MY PHILOSOPHY

"Let us begin what, where why or when will all be explained. Why is destruction a game? See I'm not insane In fact I'm kind of rational. When I be asking yo who is more dramatical?" "My Philosophy" Boogie Down Production.

It was **1988**, time to set it straight, ain't no half-steppin. I was at one of the coolest high schools in New Orleans, **Alcee Fortier**. While I was at the library one day, I haphazardly ran into an interesting story from a Times-Picayune microfiche. The story was about a brother named **Mark Essex**. He was a **Navy** veteran from Emporia, Kansas living in New Orleans. Essex was also a member of the **Black Panther Party**. He allegedly went on a crime spree that lasted several days. According to the Times-Picayune, Mr. Essex was upset over the murder of two innocent brothers by NOPD officers. His alleged crime spree started on **December 31, 1972**. It ended **January 7, 1973**, after the police killed him atop the **Howard Johnson's** hotel. In the aftermath, it was alleged that he shot 19 people, including ten police officers. Many attributed his crime spree to racism white supremacy. While serving in the United States Navy, he endured an unprecedented amount of racism. Mr. Essex had mental issues, and a psychiatrist should have assessed him. As I mentioned, this is the psychological effect that racism can have on us.

November 19, 1986, Larry Davis of the **Bronx** clapped six NYPD police officers. The officers were attempting to execute an illegal raid at his sister's home. They tried to raid the home to question him about a murder, but Mr. Davis eluded capture then managed to evade a search for 17 days. He was brought to trial then acquitted for shooting the police officers. He was also acquitted of the murders they raided the home to question him about. The state eventually found him guilty of another murder and several weapons violations. He was sentenced to **25 to life. February 20, 2008,** he was killed by another inmate at the Shawangunk Correctional Facility in Ulster County, New York.

To the black community, these two stories are like folklore. They send the message that not all black men will take shit from the police. That year NWA dropped one of the most prolific albums of that era, **"Straight Outta Compton."** The album told the story of life in the streets of Los Angeles by fed- up young black men. The most controversial song on the album was **"Fuck The Police."** They articulated the angst we've been feeling about the police for years. Performing this song bought scrutiny upon them from law enforcement.

Everyone knows the police have always been disrespectful to the black community. The "war on drugs" created a police state in **South Central, Compton, Watts,** and **Long Beach**. LAPD was using battering rams to knock over suspected crack houses. There were many complaints about excessive force. Similar to the Panthers, NWA scared the hell out of white America. They feared that their music would trigger violence. But since when has the European cared about violence?

I started hearing about all kinds of sophisticated weapons like Uzi's, Llamas, Mossberg's, Tech Nines, and Ak-47's (we call them choppers). How does an Uzi made in Israel get into **New Orleans, Los Angeles, Chicago, Miami, Washington D.C.,** or **New York**? President Reagan was always on television talking about arms control, but what type of "arms control" allows Russian-made assault rifles into the hood? These weapons were made for combat; these youngsters aren't trained to handle them. This is why shootings often end in innocent fatalities.

The criminal element had taken siege, and it became unsafe for kids to play outside. It was amazing that so much crime existed in the neighborhood despite all the police presence. Those that attempted to do anything about it were suppressed or even killed. The police were failing us; most crimes were investigated poorly or not at all. Some in law enforcement took pleasure in seeing people killed that they could not prosecute. **Tupac Shakur** once said, **"the same criminal element that the white community is afraid of the black community is afraid of it too."** What makes the government think that we desire to be among the killers, rapists, stick-up kids, paedophiles, gang bangers, and con men? How come the aggressive tactics used to keep their communities free of crime aren't replicated in ours? **Is this a conspiracy or a plan?**

"And then you realize we don't care. We don't just say no, we too busy saying yeah! About drinking straight out of the eight bottles. Do I look like a mother fucking role model? To a kid looking up to me life ain't nothing but bitches and money." "Gangsta, Gangsta" NWA.

How did crime get into our communities? To chronicle this, I had to go way back to **1933**. This was when **Ellsworth "Bumpy" Johnson** became the first major black crime figure in America. Bumpy Johnson was a native of **North Carolina;** he was an associate and part-time bodyguard to **Stephanie St. Clair.** Madame St. Clare was the unquestioned leader of the Harlem number rackets. The numbers were a game of chance; a series of numbers would come out daily from a designated area, usually a newspaper. If you had the winning numbers, you won money based on the percentage you wagered. This is where the idea came from to do the lottery. Running numbers was a lucrative business, although it was illegal, especially in Harlem. Law enforcement never gets interested in number runners; they mostly stayed under the radar. Eventually, word got out about how much money they were making in Harlem. This caught the attention of Mafia boss **Arthur Flegenheimer**. Flegenheimer was from **Germany;** he's well known as **Dutch Schultz**. Eager to cash in on this lucrative business, he moved into Harlem then forcibly acquired most of the operations of the number.

While attempting to supplant Madame St. Claire, he became engaged in a war with Bumpy Johnson. No one could have imagined that Bumpy Johnson would go toe to toe with one of the most feared Mafia bosses of that era. This is another example of white privilege. Blacks couldn't even have illegal businesses without someone white trying to take them away from them. Despite the number of brothers killed on both sides, Bumpy Johnson emerges victoriously. This made him a legend in Harlem and a model of success for brothers in the streets. **July 7, 1968,** Bumpy Johnson died of heart failure; he was only 62 years old.

By that time, **Leroy "Nicky" Barnes** had risen to power. A native of Harlem, he beat a heroin addiction to become a major drug lord. It's been rumored that the character **Priest Ron O'Neil** portrayed in **"SuperFly"** was modeled after him. He was the first to set up a legit drug crew. His organization infrastructure was similar to the Mafia. They called themselves **"The Council"** adopting an oath based on honor, trust, and loyalty. Like a Mafia boss, when he was arrested, he evaded prosecution. Mr. Barnes made it to the front cover of the New York Times, where they labeled him **"Mr. Untouchable."** All of this caught the attention of President **Jimmy Carter**. In Outraged, he demanded that Nicky Barnes be bought up on charges. In **1978** Nicky Barnes and his associates were convicted of running a criminal conspiracy, drug distribution, weapons, and murder. After he was convicted, he became upset over disloyalty from his crew. Most of the disloyalty surrounded his wife dating another member of the council.

That's when he decided to turn state witness for the government. Through his cooperation, an additional **44 arrests** were made. That resulted in **16 more convictions**. After serving **35 years,** he was released into witness protection.

In the mid-**1980,** the **"new jack hustler"** emerged. **Azie "AZ" Faison, Richard "Rich" Porter,** and **Alberto "Alpo" Martinez** became the standard by which most dealers are judged. In Harlem, these young men had an incredible rise in the crack trade. They were treated like rap stars, but they owned all those luxury items you often hear rappers brag about. Their narcotic business caused much harm in the community costing dozens of lives with many brothers imprisoned. Richard Porter and his 12-year-old brother William were unfortunate victims of their shady dealings. **December 5, 1989,** the young William Porter was kidnapped. He was held pending a paid ransom. The kidnappers sent one of his fingers to his family to extort the money. On **January 4, 1990,** Rich Porter was found dead in the Bronx; a few weeks later, they found William just a mile away. Faison left the game after an attempt on his life by some goons who robbed him. After Alpo was arrested, he surprised everyone when he agreed to cooperate with the government. He gave up information on several of his associates implicating himself and others in various crimes. The most shocking of all was his confession to the murder of Rich Porter.

These brothers were enterprising, charismatic, savvy, courageous, dedicated, charming, adventurous, and romantic. They were also ruthless, psychotic, cruel, intimidating, manipulative, and unsympathetic. Despite their popularity or money, all of these brothers ended up in unfortunate situations. Snitching on your partners in crime for less time had become part of the game. Prosecutors knew this move could nullify the game. They successfully used this tactic, and conviction rates soared. They know there's no honor among thieves. When this didn't work, they threatened to incarcerate the family members. This practice is common among prosecutors. What is being done to monitor such a powerful office?

December 6, 1984, Raymond Liuzza is shot and killed after being robbed around the corner from his home. While still conscious, he describes his assailant as an African American male. On **December 8, 1984,** acting on a tip, NOPD officers arrested two men **John Thompson** and **Kevin Freeman**. Both men were booked with arm robbery and murder. The two men's photos were plastered all over the Times-Picayune newspaper and on several local news channels. After seeing Mr. Thompson's face on the news, a family that survived a carjacking claimed he fit the description of the carjacker. The D.A. then charged him with carjacking. He was tried for carjacking first on **April 4, 1985.** He was convicted of carjacking then sentenced to **49 years**. Kevin Freeman agreed to testify against him in the armed robbery and murder trial that was held later. According to prosecutors, Thompson had the murder weapon and a ring taken from Mr. Liuzza. Freeman claimed Thompson and himself robbed Liuzza then shot him. Most of the witnesses disputed his account, claiming that only one man was seen fleeing the scene. **May 8, 1985,** Thompson was found guilty of murder and arm robbery then sentenced to death. While he was on death row, he appealed his case several times, but by **1999** his execution date had been set. In April of the same year, investigators working with his legal defense team discovered blood tested from the carjacking scene did not match his. They found this out just thirty days before he was scheduled to be executed. His defense team learned the DA willfully withheld this evidence. Prosecutors admitted to wrongdoing then dismissed the charges.

Investigators found a lot of misconduct in his cases. The misconduct included witnesses being paid reward money by the victim's family. In **July 2002,** the **Louisiana Fourth Circuit Court of Appeal** overturned Mr. Thompson's murder conviction. The court remanded his carjacking case to a retrial on **May 8, 2003.** A jury acquitted him of the carjacking then he was immediately released. In **2008** he won a lawsuit that he filed against the district attorney's office of New Orleans. The jury awarded him **14 million** dollars. The verdict was appealed up to the Supreme Court. Justice

Clarence Thomas, one dissenting vote, overturned it. In his brief, he stated that the District Attorney's office didn't present a pattern of misconduct. He never researched that, or he would have discovered a pattern of corruption, not only by the district attorney office of New Orleans but throughout the United States.

July 3, **1996,** 17-year-old **Shareef Cousins** became the youngest person sentenced to death in Louisiana. The young Mr. Cousins was convicted of the murder and arm robbery of **Michael Gerardi**. The crime occurred in the **French Quarters** while Gerardi was on a date. Connie Babin, his date that evening, identified Mr. Cousins as the trigger man. This is despite having notoriously bad eyesight. On the night of the murder, she wasn't wearing her prescription contact lenses or her glasses. She only identified Mr. Cousins, although she testified that he had accomplices. This trial was marred in misconduct, including coerced witnesses, prosecutors kidnapping witnesses, and suppressed evidence. They even had a homicide detective collect money from the crime stoppers tip leading to his arrest.

In **January** of **1998,** the Louisiana Supreme Court granted him a new trial. The new trial was based on the discovery that the prosecution withheld evidence. The district attorney's office withheld a videotape of Mr. Cousins playing in a basketball game at the time of the murder. A few months later, district attorney **Harry Connick** dropped the case then scheduled his release. In June of 2005, prosecutor **Roger Jordan** was disciplined by the Louisiana Supreme Court for his role. He was given a three-year suspended sentence. This was a slap on the wrist for plotting to kill an innocent young black man. I can talk about more stories like this, but it would fill up this entire book.

How many innocent people languish in prison behind shady prosecutors? Where's the government agency responsible for monitoring this? The legislative, executive and judicial branches were supposedly set up to provide a system of checks and balances. My history books taught me each branch was set up so that one individual branch doesn't usurp its power. Is all of this just a theory? All of these brothers were giving negative media coverage that damaged their hopes of getting a fair trial. **Public Enemy** said, **"Don't Believe The Hype."**

"Used abused without clues I refused to blow a fuse they even had it on the news." "Don't Believe The Hype" Public Enemy.

1988 was arguably the best year ever for Hip Hop. Many classic albums were released like **Public Enemy "It Takes A Nation Of Millions To Hold Us Back," EPMD "Strictly Business," Slick Rick "The Great Adventures Of Slick Rick," Run-Dmc "Tougher Than Leather," NWA "Straight Outta Compton," King Tee "Act A Fool," Boogie Down Productions "By Any Means Necessary," Marly Marl "In Control Vol 1," Eazy E "Eazy Duz It," Dougie Fresh "The Greatest Entertainer," Eric B and Rakim "Follow The Leader," Big Daddy Kane "Long Live The Kane," Ultramagnectic MC's "Critical Beatdown," MC Shan "Born To Be Wild," Ice-T "Power," Jazzy Jeff and The Fresh Prince "He's The Dj I'm The Rapper," The Jungle Brothers "Straight Out The Jungle," The Geto Boys "Making Trouble," Schoolly D "Smoke Some Kill", Kid N Play "2 Hype", Biz Markie "Goin Off," The Audio Two "What More Can I Say?," Salt N Pepa "Salt With A Deadly Pepa" Mantronix "In Full Effect"** and **Mc Lyte "Lyte As A Rock."**

MC Lyte is a very talented female rapper from **Brooklyn**. She is arguably the most influential female MC in the history of Hip Hop. She came on the scene banging with her classic single **"Paper Thin."** MC Lyte mega female rap group Salt N Pepa and Roxanne Shante showed that female emcees had arrived. This was an interesting variety; there was an incredible amount of balance. What allowed this balance was the diversity of MCs and their producers.

Mr. Petticore was helping me to become a better writer. My editorials had become a must-read. I was elected class president, a position I never relinquished. I had a tight schedule my D.E. class kept me busy. I attended most of the athletic events because I wrote some of the sports articles, and I still worked at TCA. Most of us were athletes, in the band, on one of the marching teams, or in some club. These extracurricular activities kept us busy, leaving little time for mischief.

The friends I gained at Fortier were like my brothers. I still communicate with most of them—shots out to **Edward**, **Corey**, **Leonard**, **Yusuf,** and **Johnathan**. My distributive education class was important. D.E. taught us business skills like accounting and bookkeeping. The program was designed to teach skills needed to be a business owner. D.E. students were required to dress professionally like in corporate America. Friday was our only casual day and some holidays. Monday thru Thursday, we wore slacks, dress shirts, ties, and dress shoes. The sisters wore professional dresses or pants suits. To be in this class, you had to be employed. Part of our grade was based on job performance. **Mr. Brown** was our D.E. teacher; he was the perfect person to teach this program. I placed him on my list of teachers that excelled. He was a great mentor and a good motivator who taught us business skills, showing us an alternative to poverty. I understand he could have been out making lots of money, but he was there teaching us. D.E. held conventions where we competed in sales, management, marketing, and business procedures. We always represented Fortier and Mr. Brown well. We did a lot of work in the community, like visiting the elderly and buying Christmas presents for sick children. Most of us only had a few classes so after school we usually went to work.

That year I did something that I would regret. **Mr. Cook,** my chemistry teacher, was known as somebody not to be played with. He had no problem with flunking your ass if you failed to take his class seriously. When class schedules came out, everyone prayed they didn't get him. My prayers went unanswered. Mr. Cook was a different breed; no jive worked on him. After a few weeks, I couldn't keep up. Chemistry was mandatory; not passing would mean trouble. So I manipulated my counselor to remove me from his class. Once I informed him, I could see the disappointment in his eyes. It's not like students didn't always find ways to get out of his class. I think he expected better of me. The complaints were that Mr. Cook was too demanding, wasn't flexible, and he taught like a college professor. If a lot of us had known better, we would have embraced that challenge. Mr. Cook was only trying to prepare us for the future. We should have had more teachers like him, but Fortier was such a cool ass school.

In **1988** rap artists were stepping up to many challenges, but some were tough. **August 27, 1987, Scott "Scott La Rock" Sterling** is shot and killed in the Bronx. DJ Scott La Rock of **Boogie Down Productions** had been murdered. **Scott La Rock** becomes the first high-profile rap artist murdered. It took a while for this news to get out around the nation, but it shocked the world of Hip Hop when it did. As the Hip Hop community mourned his loss, many in the movement wondered how it would affect Hip Hop? More importantly, how would Boogie Down Productions survive? Their response was brilliant. **"By All Means Necessary"** was a bona fide classic. **KRS-One** transforms himself from a gangsta to a philosopher; it was incredible. It was an outstanding album showcasing a mature **KRS-One** infusing consciousness into their music. Nobody knows if the loss of Scott La Rock was the epiphany behind his dramatic transformation, but we know Hip Hop benefitted.

"It Takes A Nation Of Millions To Hold Us Back" is arguably the greatest album in the history of Hip Hop. **Public Enemy** comes with a level of consciousness in rap music not seen since. **"The Bomb Squad"** set a historical production style and musicianship. The revolutionary spirit was evident. P.E. takes us back to the days of the black power movement. Through their music, we became soldiers of the same struggle. With all of our past great heroes, **Chuck D** takes us on a visit while introducing us to some.

"Farrakhan's a prophet that I think you better listen to, what he can say to you is what you ought to do." "Bring Da Noise" Public Enemy.

Minister Louis Farrakhan has been the Nation Of Islam leader since 1978, but before Chuck D mentioned his name, I had never heard of the man. The Nation Of Islam originated in 1930 under The Honorable Elijah Muhammad (The Messenger Of Allah). The Nation Of Islam doctrine came from the teachings of Master Fard Muhammad (Allah In Person), who came to the wilderness of North America in search of the lost tribe of Shabazz. Often referred to as "the black muslins," the NOI displays a high discipline level. This type of discipline was rare in the black community. They were intelligent with great business acumen. The program includes a healthy diet with a rigorous required study, prayer, and fasting. Under the leadership of The Honorable Elijah Muhammad, the NOI rose to prominence.

Malcolm X, the most recognizable person ever associated with the NOI, has been an inspiration to many. He was a strong influence on the black power movement. As the national spokesman of the NOI, Malcolm X rose to prominence. Dr. Khalid Muhammad, the founding chairman of the New Black Panther Party, served as the national assistant to Minister Farrakhan. He eventually became the NOI national spokesman. The NOI have reformed many brothers and sisters. Their success in cleaning people of immoral or criminal behavior has become legendary. The NOI was certainly needed in my community. My neighborhood was full of addicts, dealers, and harlots. Any kind of reform would have been welcomed.

The NOI business acumen was unbridled. During their heyday, they owned various businesses, including fish markets, bakeries, and restaurants. They are famous for the bean pies that they sell on street corners nationwide. They even published a newspaper named The Final Call.

Later on, I heard some of Farrakhan's speeches, and I found the brother inspiring. I've attended several of his events. He's a brilliant man and an eloquent speaker. He inspired one million black men to join him for a day of atonement in Washington D.C. I shouldn't have to hear about him on a **Public Enemy** record. **Is it a conspiracy or a plan?**

Allowing Europeans and some misinformed black people to determine our leaders is a mistake. Somehow this kind of mentality has been ingrained in us. It hinders us as it lies within our psyche. It stays there, lingering and eventually finding its way into our souls. Those demons must be exorcised. What if **Chuck D** had never mentioned **Farrakhan** or **Joann Chesimard?**

"Hard my calling card recorded and ordered supporter of Chesimard."
"Rebel Without A Pause" Public Enemy.

Assata Shakur, formerly Joann Chesimard, was a **Black Panthers** and the **Black Liberation Army** member. In **May of 1973,** she was charged with the murder of New Jersey state trooper Werner Foerster and assaulting his partner James Harper. According to reports, things got out of control after fellow **BLA** members **Sundiata Acoli** and **Zayd Malik Shakur** were pulled over for a traffic stop. A confrontation ensued, causing the death of the trooper. Ms. Shakur was shot twice, and Zayd Malik Shakur, who later died of his injuries. While she was rehabbed from her injuries, she was subjugated to harsh abuse in the New Jersey correctional institution. She detailed it all in her autobiography **"Assata." November 2**, **1979,** she managed to escape from Clinton Correctional Facility For Women. Since then, she has remained in exile.

Rap artists like **Public Enemy** and **Boogie Down Productions** opened us up to a side of American history that many wanted to remain hidden. The conscious rap movement was instilling self-pride in us, raising our consciousness. Their songs were teaching us a proper understanding of the struggles of our forefathers. That is the history that wasn't taught to us by some of our elders or in school. What were the powers that be feared? We got a healthy dosage of Alexander, the not- so-great, and others like him. Wasn't Alexander a murderer as they claim Assata was? He was the leader of a group that overthrew a government. This is what they claim the Panthers were trying to do. So the department of education determines who and what is criminal?

"Jeffrey Dahmer enters the room without cuffs. How the hell do we get stuffed in the back of a cell on an isle ain't it wild? What's a criminal?" **"Hazy Shade Of Criminal" Public Enemy.**

The black history we were taught started with slavery and ended with Jim Crow. I'm in high school, but I feel like I'm going backward. I think my world history teacher Mrs. Johnson knew this was some bullshit. She always had some sly comments that many people ignored. She is the one I got the saying **"Egyptians mysteriously moved out of Africa"** from. This all helped to further my belief in a conspiracy. Information was being kept away from us on purpose, which we wouldn't even know had it not been for rap music.

"It's like teaching a dog to be a cat you don't teach white kids to be black." "Why Is That?" Boogie Down Productions.

I learned that FBI director **J. Edgar Hoover** implemented a counterintelligence program. He used federal agents to infiltrate groups he considered a threat to national security. Once the agents were inside, they used the information gathered against them. These federal agents committed felonious acts that resulted in weakening the organization. These covert acts caused the loss of lives, property, and plenty of prison convictions. It causes tremendous damage to the organization's reputation, the people involved and anyone connected.

Media outlets picked up on these tactics persecuting brothers in the public's eyes. This makes finding an impartial jury impossible. The media constantly cast negative stereotypes of us even if we are the victims. A jury often convicts us based on public opinion. There are lots of stereotypes of the black man.

According to the recent census, there are approximately **44 million** black people in America. For the sake of argument, half of them are males (we know there are more females). That's approximately **22 million black men**. Here are some examples: **(A) There are more black men in prison than in college**. At the date of this writing, the department of education estimates approximately **1.4 million** black men enrolled in colleges and universities. The department of corrections estimates there are approximately **837,000** black men incarcerated. I know that number is high, and it probably will increase by the time you read this but so will the enrollment rate for black males in college. **(B) Most black men are on drugs**. In the US, this stereotype has been instrumental in influencing drug policy. According to the NAACP study on the US criminal justice system, blacks represent **12%** of total drug users. For the sake of argument, let's say that the whole 12% represents black males only (we know there are some sisters in that number). That would be approximately **2,640,000,000** black men. **(C) A lot of black men are gay or closet homosexuals**. The term used to describe this class of brothers is "down low." Recent studies conducted by the gay and lesbian community have estimated approximately 2% of black men in America are homosexual. That's around **440,000** black men. This stereotype originated with disgruntled black feminists. They used it when complaining of no desirable black men. The total sum of black men that society deems flawed is **3,917,000,000** out of approximately **22 million.** This certainly isn't all or most, as some suggest. These numbers are actually lower. I purposely excluded black females from some. This should debunk the theory that black men are intractable as depicted. Unfortunately, with all the misinformation on our people, misinformed blacks share in perpetuating these lies.

Louisiana has a history of biracial affairs. French slave owners frequently rape black women. From this violation, some of these women bore children. The mixture of the two ethnicities produced a unique group of people who came to be known as Creoles. As the females grew older, some of them were taken as concubines. Some slave owners lived double lives with their white wives and children, then doing the same with their Creole concubines. After a while, these affairs were arranged by the families. They had extravagant balls where Frenchmen would gather to meet Creole women for this designated purpose. **Anne Rice** wrote a novel about it named **"The Feast Of All Saints."** In **2001** a movie of the same-titled was released.

Most Creoles were not easily identifiable because of the hue of their skin. To avoid discrimination, some of them passed for white. They benefited from their slave master fathers, who gave them resources to develop their own communities. Some Creoles even owned slaves. Some were educated; most of them took great interest in the fine arts. Most Creoles considered themselves elite because of their white ancestry. This caused a tremendous amount of conflict, promoting the separation we sometimes see today. The famous debate between **Booker T. Washington** and **WEB Dubois** was rumored to be about their different skin hues as their differences in philosophies.

Dark skin and light skin blacks get the same treatment from Europeans. Look at how many of them are killed by the police or incarcerated. What's disturbing is that this still plays a role in New Orleans, especially in politics. It may be why New Orleans never had a dark skin mayor. Uniting is the answer to black people; it may be the only way to achieve true freedom.

"Broken down to the very last compound, see how it sounds a little un rational. A lot of MCs love to use the word dramatical." "My Philosophy" Boogie Down Productions.

CHAPTER 6

SOUND OF DA POLICE

"Ya hotshot, wanna get props and be a savior first show a little respect,change your behavior" "Sound Of Da Police" Krs One

It's **1989,** my senior year. I kept the fresh cameo cut every day. I was determined to make my final year of high school a good one. I was surprised I had made it this far now I was determined to finish. I figured it would be senseless to come all this way only to quit. This was despite knowing I wasn't receiving a quality education. If I decided to attend college, I would have to repeat some of the same steps. I was in a bad situation, so I had to make the possible best out of it.

I was still focused on being a better writer, so I started to take English seriously. Mrs. Picou was my English teacher the previous year and required us to read two books. I didn't think much about them at the time. Maybe I was so used to being Europeanized I never gave it much thought. Sometimes I just dealt with the hustle of trying to make the grade. I always use the summer to reflect on the previous year. The first book was **"The Red Badge Of Courage"** written by **Stephen Crane**. The book was about Henry Fleming, a soldier fighting in the Civil War for the Union army. He's Afraid to fight, so he goes awol. He eventually rejoins his regiment then desperately tries to sustain an injury. He wanted "a red badge of courage" to quell his cowardice. The other book was **"The Catcher In The Rye,"** written by **J.D. Salinger**. The Catcher In The Rye follows the life of Holden Caulfield, a student at Pencey Prep, a fictional private school in Pennsylvania. He's a gregarious teenager who smokes, drinks, hangs out all night, and cusses like an adult. He's irresponsible, obnoxious, and disrespectful. Salinger added humor throughout the book. I was perplexed why she required us to read these two books? I learned nothing from a coward or a privileged white kid. There were plenty of great black authors to select from, like **Richard Wright, Langston Hughes, Toni Morrison, James Baldwin, Frances Cress Welsing**, and **Zora Neal Hurston.**

Free Enterprise was another interesting subject Mrs. Quinn taught this class. She was a good teacher, and many who attended Fortier can verify that. She would visit her student's homes to meet their parents. Free Enterprise taught us the system used in America that gives each of its citizens the means to attain life, liberty, and the pursuit of happiness. All of this sounds great; however, these principles seem to be limited to certain groups of people.

How many potential black business owners have been turned down for loans while white's in the same position were approved? How many Ex-felons are denied jobs regardless of the nature of their crimes? How many black children can't complete college because they were denied student loans or grants? If this is a free enterprise, I sure would hate to pay for it.

Meanwhile, the murder rate in New Orleans continued to climb. People that I knew had gotten killed. Many in the community wondered why the police aren't doing anything. What hadn't been discovered was how corrupt the **New Orleans** police department was. There were rumors about certain police officers that came in the hood to wreak havoc. They were rumored to take certain suspected criminals under the Broad overpass then rob them of drugs, personal property, or money. These incidents went unreported because most of the victims were alleged criminals. They didn't want to expose themselves to that type of scrutiny.

On **October 13, 1994,** the misdeeds of the NOPD would be exposed. The murder of **Kim Groves,** a 31-year-old single mother of three, would conclude a lengthy investigation into corruption inside the department. Ms. Groves' murder was ordered in retaliation to a brutality complaint she filed against NOPD officer **Len Davis.** The murder plot was captured on recordings made available by federal agents.

The FBI was conducting a covert investigation on officer Davis, his partner Sammie Williams, and other NOPD officers. The investigation centered on NOPD officers who were involved in distributing drugs. In a federal investigation that spanned over ten months, it was discovered that officer Davis was the head of this drug trafficking crew. According to the FBI officer, Davis was tipped off about the complaint by someone inside the department. After learning the complaint, he arranged for trigger man Paul "Cool" Hardy to murder her. **April 27, 1996,** officer Davis was convicted of capital murder, civil rights violations, and running a drug protection racket. He was subsequently sentenced to death. Paul "Cool" Hardy was given the same sentence a few months later.

March 4, 1995, NOPD officer Antoinette Frank and her boyfriend Roger LaCaze kill three people after sticking up the Kim Anh restaurant in **New Orleans East. Cuong Vu 17, Ha Vu 24,** and fellow NOPD officer **Ronald Williams** are gunned down in the attempted armed robbery. Officers Williams and Frank were partners; both worked a paid detail at the restaurant. According to reports, officer Frank became acquainted with LaCaze after he was shot during a failed drug deal. The two became engaged in an illicit affair that lasted until the day of the murders. It was reported that during their inappropriate relationship LaCaze sometimes accompanied officer Frank on police calls.

She even allowed him to drive around in her police unit. Ms. Frank was allowed to join the force despite being caught lying on her application and failing the psychological exam twice. **July 21, 1995**, LaCaze was found guilty of capital murder and armed robbery then sentenced to death. On **October 20, 1995**, Antoinette Frank's trial was held. She was found guilty then sentenced to death. This made her the only woman on death row in Louisiana. A few months later, the remains of her missing father were found underneath the home they shared.

April 7, 1968, 17-year-old Bobby Hutton of the Black Panther Party is killed by **Oakland police**. The police shot Mr. Hutton as he exited a vacant house half- naked to show them he was unarmed.

December 4, 1969, Fred Hampton, chairman of the **Chicago** chapter of the Black Panther Party and **Mark Clark** are killed in a raid by the **Chicago police department**. At the time of his untimely death, Mr. Hampton was asleep at the side of his pregnant girlfriend Deborah Johnson. According to reports, FBI informant **William O'Neal** slipped a powerful barbiturate into their drinks, causing both men to pass out. With plans of the home supplied by FBI informant **Roy Mitchell**, the Chicago PD raided the home at 4 am.

Fred Hampton was a prolific member of the Black Panther Party. His work in the BPP helped to unify gangs, poor white folks, and Latinos. The people familiar with the Hampton and Clark's murder described the incident as an execution.

On **October 21, 2008, Jon Burge,** a **Chicago police commander**, was arrested by the FBI. Officer Burge was booked for obstruction of justice and perjury. In an FBI investigation, it was discovered that he tortured more than **200** alleged criminals, forcing them into false confessions. Officer Burge worked as a military policeman while serving in the Army during the Vietnam War. The Army trained him in the methods of torture that he used as a member of the Chicago police department. After these findings, many of the alleged confessions were vacated, and some inmates were released. In the wake of these investigations, Illinois Governor George Ryan declared a moratorium on the death penalty. The details of these incidents are in a book written by **John Conroy** titled **"Unspeakable Acts, Ordinary People: The Dynamics Of Torture."**

May 13, 1985, the **Philadelphia police department** dropped a bomb on the house occupied by MOVE members. MOVE was an Africa-centered organization founded by **John Africa**. The police had been in dispute with the organization concerning city zone violations. According to reports, the Philadelphia police department used a helicopter to drop C-4, a powerful explosive on top of the home. As the house burned down, the police prevented the fire department from putting out the blaze. Eleven people were killed, including founding member **John Africa, five children,** and **five other adults. Ramona** and **Birdie Africa** were the only survivors of the bombing. Including the home that MOVE occupied, the bomb burned down **61 homes** on **Osage Avenue.**

On March 3, 1991, several LAPD officers were shown beating motorist Rodney King on a secretly recorded video. The video sent shock waves around the nation. LAPD is busted on video using excessive force. Black people always complained about this kind of police misconduct but never had there been such conclusive evidence. After lawyers for the accused cops successfully argued for a change of venue, the trial took place in **Simi Valley. April 29, 1992,** all four officers charged were found not guilty. The verdict prompted widespread rioting in Los Angeles that lasted for three days. Rappers like Ice Cube, Ice T, NWA, and Paris predicted this would happen. The riots were the direct result of the people's frustration.

February 4, 1999, Amadou Diallo, an immigrant of Guinea, is killed as he exited a building in the Bronx. Plainclothes **NY PD** officers claim they mistook Mr. Diallo for a serial rape suspect. In an attempt to identify himself, he tried to retrieve his wallet. This prompted the police to fire **41 rounds,** mortally wounding him. The officers were part of the New York street crimes unit that has since been defunct. All four officers involved in the shooting were found not guilty in a trial held in Albany, NewYork.

On September 2, **2005**, 4 days after hurricane **Katrina Henry Glover** was gunned down by **NOPD** officer David Warren. Allegedly officer Warren was protecting a strip mall located in **Algiers**. He fired the fatal shot from atop a building several yards away with his personally owned .223 caliber rifle. The fired projectile struck Mr. Glover in the chest. After he was shot, his brother **Edward King** flagged down **William Tanner** for assistance. The two men placed Mr. Glover in the back of Mr. Tanner's Chevy Malibu then drove off to get him medical attention. They ended up at Habans Elementary School, where a make-shift police station was set up. It seemed like a safe place to take him since law enforcement officers were there. Once they arrived, they were immediately handcuffed and beaten while Mr. Glover bled to death inside the vehicle. In court proceedings, it was stated that officer Greg McRae drove off in the vehicle then set it ablaze along the levee. When Mr. Glover's charred remains were taken to the coroner's office, his head was missing. New Orleans coroner Frank Minyard refused to classified his death. The newly-elected coroner Jeffery Rouse has since classified his death as a homicide; however, the district attorney hasn't brought forth any additional charges. Henry Glover's head has never been recovered.

March 31, **2011**, officer Warren was convicted of violating Mr. Glover's federal civil rights then sentenced to **25 years**. Officer Greg McRae was convicted of obstructing justice and civil rights violations then sentenced to **17** years. A host of NOPD officers were bought up on various charges, including falsifying documents, civil rights violations, and lying to a federal grand jury.

On December 11, 2013, David Warren was acquitted in a retrial that his lawyers successfully argued for. This is disturbing, considering he testified under oath that he killed Mr. Glover and was found guilty. How many times do we hear of people who spend decades in prison before being acquitted? John Thompson came within 30 days of being executed before he was acquitted.

September 4, 2005, James Brissette (17) and **Ronald Madison (40)** are killed by **NOPD officers** while seeking higher ground after Hurricane Katrina. The incident took place atop the **Danziger Bridge**. In the mass shooting, four other people were seriously wounded. According to reports, several officers rushed to the area amid a false report from the dispatcher of an officer down. The four officers involved claimed as they arrived, four gunmen fired at them from atop the bridge. This caused their deadly reaction using assault weapons and shotguns. Ronald Madison, a developmentally disabled man, was shot in the back while attempting to flee. **April 4, 2012**, all four officers were found guilty of civil rights violations, falsifying documents, and criminal conspiracy.

Since that day, the officers have been granted retrials. The retrials were granted upon discovering that federal prosecutors discredited them by posting blogs on Nola.com. Investigators discovered that **Sal Perricone** and **Jan Mann,** two of the state's top prosecutors, posted blogs about cases they were handling. What would make Perricone and Mann violate ethics rules by participating in an online blog? How many prosecutors do this to sway public opinion? In the wake of this discovery, **Louisiana Attorney General Jim Letten** was forced to resign. Many people speculated on how much he knew about the blogs or participated?

November 21, 2006, in Atlanta, Ga, Katherine Johnston (92) is being killed by undercover **Atlanta police officers** in a home she lived in for **17** years. The officers involved were attempting to raid her home, where allegedly drugs were sold. According to reports, the police cut off burglar bars then busted down her door while executing a "no-knock" warrant. Mrs. Johnston was startled by the invasion, so she fired one shot from her revolver. After which, **39 shots** were fired back, striking her six times. In the investigation following the shooting, it was discovered that the police planted drugs in her home. They learned that the documents stating that drugs were being sold from her home had been falsified. The three officers involved, Jason Smith, Arthur Tesler, and Greg Junnier pleaded guilty to several charges, including lying to investigators, federal civil rights violations, manslaughter, and perjury.

March 7, 2012, while raiding a home in Gentilly, **20-year-old Wendell Allen,** a star basketball player, is shot and killed. **NOPD** officer Joshua Colclough fired a single shot into Mr. Allen, causing his untimely death. Mr. Allen was unarmed and wasn't wearing a shirt when the fatal shot was fired. A videotape of the raid was recorded by the police that showed details of the incident. Five children were inside the home when the police raided it, allegedly searching for marijuana. In **August** of **2013**, officer Colclough pleaded guilty to manslaughter when he was sentenced to only **four** years.

There are too many incidents like this. I could fill up this entire book with more. This is not even a microcosm of what really goes on. There's a historical disconnect between the police and the black community. Why would any police department be so desperate to hire policemen like these? They commit murder and armed robberies, falsify documents, lie to federal investigators, and plant evidence. They violate people's civil rights, torture innocent people into false confessions, and obstruct justice. They perjure themselves, lie on their applications, fail psychological exams, and traffic drugs. This is what you expect of a criminal, not from the police. Is this what we pay our tax dollars for?

Why aren't the influential political figures standing up to this misconduct? Where are the powerful civil rights organizations like the **NAACP** or the

Urban League? Nonviolently, Dr. King bravely took on racism white supremacy. We don't have to endure nearly as much as he did, but most of us do nothing. I will discuss this later.

I can't discuss the police department and the black community without acknowledging the **Black Panther Party**. On **October 15, 1966, Huey P.Newton** and **Bobby Seal** founded the **Black Panther Party**. Seal and Newton met at **Merritt Community College,** where they worked on various community projects. They were passionate about the condition of our people, so they developed revolutionary ideas for our liberation. In the beginning, the BPP tried to serve as a conduit between the police department and the community, but they became fed up with all the police corruption. This led to them designing a program to protect the community from rogue police officers. They developed a breakfast program for the children, health clinics, schools, educational seminars, and community forums. They assisted in improving the quality of life throughout the community. They even published a newspaper that boasted a high circulation. The BPP kept much of the criminal element away from the community. Well structured, they had a **10 point program** detailing the goals of the organization. The motto of the BPP was **"All Power To The People."**

Newton and Seal set up a highly structured organization with young people willing to achieve the objectives. Brilliant courageous young brothers and sisters like **Fred Hampton, H. Rap Brown (Jamel Al Amin), Kathleen Cleaver, Eldridge Cleaver, Geronimo Pratt, Bunchy Carter, Mark Clark, Bobby Hutton, Elaine Brown, Mumia Abu-Jamal, Kwame Toure (Stokley Carmichael), George Jackson, Sundiata Acoli, Assata Shakur,** and **Afeni Shakur.**

The BPP ideology was expounded on Black Nationalism from the examples of **Marcus Garvey, The Honorable Elijah Muhammad,** and **Malcolm X**. They plan to use that wisdom as a springboard towards liberation. They weren't a bunch of rabble-rousers; many of them were college-educated intellectual young people. They diligently studied the law when confronted by the police; they could recite the law to them by memory. The BPP was determined to find ways to liberate our people within the political, educational, and judicial system. They encouraged black people to embrace their natural beauty. That led many of us to stop using chemical products in our hair. This gave birth to **"the Afro,"** a natural hairstyle most blacks wore throughout the seventies. After successfully setting up a chapter in **Oakland,** they set up other chapters in **San Francisco, Chicago, New York, Philadelphia, New Jersey, Los Angeles, New Orleans, Detroit, Pittsburgh, Seattle, Washington D.C., Dallas, Denver, Cleveland, Baltimore, Kansas City, Omaha, San Diego,** and **Boston.**

Any American should endorse anyone willing to improve their community. However, the Panthers weren't viewed that way. **J. Edgar Hoover** declared them the number one threat to national security. He had federal agents infiltrate the group using his unconstitutional **cointelpro** program. This tactic weakened the BPP, causing them irreparable harm. The federal government can infiltrate positive organizations like the **Black Panther Party, SCLC,** and the **Nation Of Islam** but are unwilling to root out rogue police officers or shady prosecutors.

The **2nd amendment** gives every citizen the right to bear arms, but when the BPP openly carried their firearms, the Mulford Act was passed. On **May 2, 1967,** a group of armed members of the BPP marched on the California assembly protesting.

We had a program to combat police misconduct. I think we failed to see the importance of the BPP. We allowed media rhetoric and government infiltration to influence us. The BPP should have been adopted as the police force of the black community. These brothers knew everyone in the community, including their parents and children. This is another example of a solution to one of our problems.

Most of the BPP leaders were imprisoned or killed. The ones that managed to escape prison or the grave were discredited. Others abandon their ideas, and some even denounce their affiliation.

America has plenty of armed militias determined to overthrow the government. They boldly state their purposes in their newsletters or on their websites. These people arm themselves in preparation for **Armageddon**, a theory based on an inevitable race war. They stockpile weapons then teach their children to fire them. Go on YouTube you can find plenty of videos of them doing this. They organize gun shows that brazenly circumvent gun laws. While they continue to arm themselves, they set up gun buyback programs in our communities. They seek to disarm us while they heavily arm themselves. It's amazingly hypocritical.

Powerful organizations are set up by them, like the **National Rifle Association**. The NRA has persuasive lobbyists who work daily to curtail gun laws. Where was the NRA when the laws were changed in California after the BPP started carrying their firearms? Why don't they speak out against gun buyback programs that seek to disarm black and Latino communities? I know some black people will disagree with me citing the high rate of homicide but are the criminals the ones that are selling their guns back? Any criminal would be foolish to do that because murder has no statute of limitations.

Do you think the police would look the other way if one of these weapons was used in a homicide? All gun buyback programs do is bring harm to good black and Latino people. We need our firearms, considering our communities lack proper policing. What if Armageddon comes to fruition? What weapons would we have to protect ourselves? Where is the NRA when citizens who served their time aren't allowed to possess a weapon legally? That means a criminal record renders you defenseless.

1989 showed us how far the powers that be would go to cast negativity on the movement. **May 22, 1989**, in an interview with **Washington Times**

reporter **David Mills Public Enemy** Minister of Information, **Professor Griff** allegedly makes some anti-semitic comments. The paper published the interview, causing a lot of controversy for the group. The friction behind his statements caused Professor Griff to depart P.E. Some scolded Griff for his remarks while others appreciated his candor. Why are black people persecuted when we speak of the atrocities done to us by other people? Facts support much of what he allegedly said. The **Nation Of Islam** wrote a detailing book titled **"The Secret Relationship Between Blacks And Jews."** This incident showed us that rap was becoming a big business and controlled.

The truth of this would be reaffirmed when **Ice Cube** announced he was going solo. He said he was leaving **NWA,** citing a financial dispute. According to Cube, members of NWA were presented with unfair contracts by **Jerry Heller. Ruthless Records** CEO and fellow NWA member **Eazy E** hired Heller to be his business manager. What would make Eazy hire an old white dude like Heller? This group was considered anti-establishment; this surely didn't fit in with our perception. It was alleged that members of NWA were paid a meager amount of money from Ruthless multi-platinum albums **"Straight Outta Compton"** and **"Eazy Duz It."** Ice Cube was credited with writing most of both albums. He was considered the voice of NWA. How come one of the leading voices in Hip Hop isn't being compensated? We couldn't believe all of this was happening. We had no idea how this would affect NWA or Ice Cube? These two events rocked the movement. Everyone was in a tailspin caught between allegiances. Some Felt like Ice Cube had got the big head and allowed outsiders to influence him. On his album **"Death Certificate,"** he recorded **"No Vaseline,"** detailing his reasons for leaving the group.

"You can't be a nigga for life crew with a white boy telling you what to do." "No Vaseline" Ice Cube.

The sentiments were that Jerry Heller ruined one of the greatest rap groups of all time. Some argue that the same may have happened if Eazy had hired a black manager. Eazy needed to provide structure to his rapidly growing company. He didn't know much about the music business and relied on Jerry Heller's experience. White executives started to take over most rap labels, a trait they still share.

That year, **Rick Rubin**, the co-founder of **Def Jam Records,** left the label. He launched **Def American Records**. Def Jam is widely regarded as the label that represented Hip Hop to the fullest. Def Jam's impressive list of artists included **T- la Rock, Public Enemy, LL Cool J**, **The Beastie Boys, Slick Rick,** and **EPMD**. CEO **Russell Simmons** made the label prominent. As a manager, he helped guide **LL Cool J, Eric B and Rakim,** **Whodini, Stetsasonic,** and **Run-DMC** in their careers.

Ice T released his third full-length album, **"Freedom Of Speech Just Watch What You Say."** The production was different on this album. He details his struggles with censorship on songs like **"Freedom Of Speech"** and **"This One's For Me,"** a song he recorded in support of **Public Enemy**.

Southern rap artists make another huge impact after the release of **The Geto Boys "Grip It On The Next Level."** The Geto Boys hailed from **Houston's** notorious **5th ward**. The group featured **Scarface, Willie D,** and a little person from **Brooklyn** named **Bushwick Bill**. The makeup of the group is historical. There has never before been a little person featured in a rap group. Despite his size, Bushwick Bill was a good rapper. Their raw, gritty psychotic lyrics were unique. Some would brand the style of rap "horrorcore." The Geto Boys could be gangsta on songs like **"Read These Nike's"** and **"Life In The Fast Lane,"** or political on songs like **"Do It Like A G.O."** and **"No Sellout,"** a song they recorded in support of **Public Enemy. Rap A Lot** records CEO was **James Prince**, an intelligent brother from Houston. His label produced a mature brand of rap music infused with street knowledge and political activism. Houston was now contributing to the Hip Hop movement.

The 2 Live Crew's second nationally released album, **"Nasty As They Wanna Be,"** garnered a lot of publicity and opened up another debate on censorship. **Big Daddy Kane's** sophomore release **"It's A Big Daddy Thing"** solidified him among great MCs while establishing him as a sex symbol. **De La Soul's** debut album **"3ft High And Rising"** redefined Hip Hop adding to a core of balance during that era. **The Beastie Boys** follow-up album **"Paul's Boutique"** was released to critical acclaim cementing their place in Hip Hop. **Third Base** would shatter stereotypes once more with their debut album **"The Cactus"** on **Def Jam,** While **Kool G Rap and DJ Polo's "Roads To Richest"** showed the world G Rap had arrived.

The Juice Crew was coming into their own as a rap collective consisting of **Kool G Rap**, **Master Ace**, **Roxanne Shante**, **Big Daddy Kane**, **MC Shan**, **Biz Markie**, **TJ Swan**, **Tragedy Khadafi,** and **Craig G**. Under the tutelage of super producer **Marly Marl**, they started to get their props.

King Sun's debut album **"XL"** showed and proved the **Five Percent Nation's** influence on Hip Hop culture. **MC Lyte's "Eyes On This"** would cement her legendary status. She shows a tremendous amount of growth, recording an album that rivaled her male counterparts. Despite the controversy over Ice Cube leaving **Ruthless Records,** they released the **D.O.C "Nobody Can Do It Better"** to huge commercial success.

The highlight of the year was the release of **Queen Latifah's** debut album **"All Hail The Queen."** Her name spoke volumes; although few knew what it meant **(Latifah means: elegant, kind, and gentle),** we knew it had meaning. She proclaimed herself the **"Queen Of Royal Badness."**

She encompasses the lyrical skill as all her contemporaries blended with consciousness. It felt good hearing from a sister during this era. Her album cover was awesome; she looked like royalty with a map of **Africa** stamped on it. **Mark the 45 King** production was the perfect match for her style. She had an influence on many sisters in Hip Hop like **Sister Souljah, Isis, Nefertiti,** and **L. Boogie (Lauryn Hill).**

Boogie Down Productions "Ghetto Music The Blueprint Of Hip Hop" displays **Krs-One** delving rap deeper into consciousness. This classic album gave us great songs like **"Why Is That," "You Must Learn,"** and **"Jack Of Spades."** Known for his incredible cover art, this one has Krs-One sitting on the curb with a policeman harassing him. It was a reflection of how the black community felt about the cops.

To counteract the negativity attached to Hip Hop, **Krs-One** started **The Stop The Violence Movement**. He convened an impressive list of rap artists to record **"Self Destruction,"** a kind of **"We Are The World"** type of rap song. The mega single included **Krs-One, D-Nice, MC Lyte, Ms. Melodie, Kool Moe Dee, Public Enemy, Doug E Fresh, Just-Ice, Heavy D,** and **Stetsasonic.**

In **March of 2004, Miami Herald** journalist **Evelyn McDonald** discovered a covert rap intelligence unit. It started to unravel after the Miami Beach Police contacted her. The MB PD requested phone numbers and addresses of some rap artists she recently did an article on. Bewildered, she and fellow journalist **Nicole White** did some digging. They discovered that a special unit of the NYPD had been trained to survey rap artists. Former NYPD police officer **Derek Parker** had compiled a special binder on rap artists. The unique binder contained police records, mug shots, and bios on rap artists. It also contained addresses, phone numbers, license plate numbers, and other personal information. There were lyrics from all rappers they deem criminal and any beef they might have. NYPD shared the dossier with police forces nationally to watch rap artists. The documents displayed a federal seal which means that the federal government is involved.

With all the surveillance they do on rappers, how come they never solved any rapper homicide? Rap artists are known to have people in their entourages still in street life. The police ignore them while specifically targeting the rapper. No genre of music has ever come under such scrutiny. When the binder was exposed, there was no white rap artist. **Is it a conspiracy or a plan?**

The theme song of **89'** was **Public Enemy's "Fight The Power,"** which was featured throughout **Spike Lee's** movie **"Do The Right Thing."** In this classic film, Spike Lee stars as "Mookie," the pizza delivery man for Sal's Pizzeria. As he makes deliveries, he comes in contact with a host of interesting characters. Those are Bugging Out, his high-energy friend, his Puerto Rican girlfriend Tina, an older woman they call Mama sister, an alcoholic they call Da Mayor, and Radio Raheem. Everyone called him that because he carried a huge radio wherever he went. Radio Raheem was deep into Hip Hop culture; he wore a lot of trunk jewelry, and he only played Public Enemy music.

It's scorching in Brooklyn that summer, causing tension in the neighborhood. Things boil over when Bugging Out insists that Sal put some black people on the wall of his restaurant. Annoyed by his request, Sal kicks him out of the restaurant, but he returns later with Radio Raheem making the same demands. This incenses Sal to the extent that he takes out his bat and destroys Raheem's radio. Enraged, Raheem attacks Sal, and a melee starts involving himself, Bugging Out, and Sal's sons. The police are called out, and when they arrive, one of them chokes Raheem to death with a billy club. After witnessing this, the distraught crowd erupts into a riot destroying Sal's historic pizzeria. Spike Lee is from Brooklyn; he was well aware of these stories. He wasn't afraid to bring this story to the big screen.

On "Ghetto Music," Krs-One asked, **"Who Protects Us From U?"** An overwhelming amount of police officers are forgiven for some heinous crimes even if caught red-handed. The police are supposed to be public servants paid with our tax dollars. Too often, this is overlooked. We must demand to have the same rights as all Americans. As incidents of police misconduct continue, public trust is eroded. This often leads to people taking the law into their own hands. This is one of the reasons why many crimes go unreported.

Police tactics like illegal stop-and-frisk have created a fear of the public servants your tax dollars pay the salaries of. Randomly following a black person with a nice vehicle speaks volumes. It's like saying, "we aren't supposed to have nice things." Historically we have worked harder than anyone in this country, although most of it was for nothing. The police do intimidating shit to us, like surround your vehicle until you relinquish a search. This is a violation of your constitutional rights, and most of them know it.

Racial profiling started when our ancestors came upon these shores. It was "racial profiling" when the auctioneer spoke of each black person's unique features that made them attractive to slave owners. Some of us have become so inundated by the powers that be when we see a black person in the back of a police vehicle, we assume they are guilty. This shows we have developed the same attitudes about ourselves as the oppressor.

I don't want to leave this chapter without admitting that there are some honest policemen. Police commissioners like **Richard Pennington** did a great job reforming the NOPD. During his tenure, he rooted out corruption and enforced strict guidelines for hiring while securing public trust. If his directives had remained, maybe they could have avoided the embarrassment of Henry Glover and Danziger?

I know good police officers get tired of taking on this level of criticism from the public. They do a great job offering their best service to the community.

I applaud that effort, and as a veteran, I understand your level of dedication. My solution to you is to unite with like-minded police officers. Form a coalition to root out those contrary to what you swore to. The corruption must be rooted out from inside the force than not allowed to return. Many of you know some of your fellow officers cross the line but stand by and do nothing. This makes you just as guilty; their behavior reflects upon you all. Once the public starts seeing enough good policemen, maybe public trust will return. This could make any law enforcement officer's job easier. Think about how many of your investigations that go nowhere because witnesses aren't willing to come forth. This could lead to better investigations allowing key criminals to be apprehended. These police officers offer the only hope because something has to be done. We die every day at the hands of the police.

"Your laws are minimal cause you won't even think about looking at the real criminal. This has got to cease. Cause we be getting hyped to the sound of da police!" "Sound Of The Police" Krs-One.

CHAPTER 7

BROTHERS GONNA WORK IT OUT

"Uh, your bad self helped me break this down from off the shelf here's a music serving you so use it papa's got a brand new funk." "Brothers Gonna Work It Out" Public Enemy.

This chapter is a collection of critical thinking and constructive criticism. I will take a careful look at the behavior of brothers of different social and economic levels. I will demonstrate how some of us end up in the penile, dead, or in dangerous situations. I will focus on our mentality and how it affects us individually and as a whole. We are afraid to say some of these things, but this is dialogue way past its time.

As a black man, I'm uniquely qualified to say them. I might be guilty of some of these same behavior traits; after all, I am a black man. I don't consider myself superior or inferior to no brother on this planet. I didn't write this chapter to demean black men or feed into any negative stereotypes. So far, I have dealt mostly with entities outside of our community, describing how they have caused us harm. This chapter will focus on how we bring harm to ourselves. I needed to write this chapter to bring my brothers some enlightenment. Someone needed to bring attention to our negative behavior traits. I want **brothers to work it out** to be better grandfathers, fathers, brothers, uncles, and cousins.

It's still **89'** I'm wondering if I should go to college or the military? I had been meeting with a Navy recruiter for a few weeks. If I were to enlist in any branch, I would rather go there. My reason for the Navy is that sailors did a lot of traveling. I read about many places, and I thought the Navy offered me the best chance to see some of them. My brother Roosevelt was in the Navy, so that factored in. I didn't want the government placing a rifle in my hand, saying point and shoot. They sure would do that if I joined the Army or the Marines. I would rather take my chances aboard a ship. I was well disciplined, so I didn't need the military to teach me much of that. I knew outside of the benefits military personnel didn't get paid a lot. I was willing to pay for college if I decided to enroll. I scored pretty well on the ACT, so I had other options. I wasn't fortunate to be brought up in a family of wealth. I couldn't afford to take extended European vacations to find myself coming home to go to college then run the family business. I will do it the best way I can on the government's dollar. I knew I swore my life, but I thought the rewards were worth the risk a **brother was gonna work it out.** I studied the situation determining outside of the "cold war," America was at peace. I didn't see the United States coming into conflict with anyone.

Brothers were still getting arrested then getting sentenced to multiple years. **Angola** and **OPP** (Orleans Parish Prison) were becoming a second home to many brothers. Judges were given time out like football numbers.

Being a black man in America is difficult; only black men can attest that it's a unique experience. Often we are discriminated against, racially profiled, and we remain targets of law enforcement. We are loved worldwide for our style, athleticism, masculine features, brilliant minds, musicianship, and colorful personalities. What's unique about us is we are hated for some of those same things.

We come from a culture of people that have historically enjoyed wealth. The Egyptians wore gold on their heads, necks, hands, wrist, and in their mouths as we do now. They had gold and diamond mines where they extracted the materials for their jewelry. They dressed in the finest linens, wools, satins, and silks. The desire for the finer things is inside our collective DNA. The Egyptians are just one example; there were many before them. Greece invaded Egypt then the European systematically acquired all of those resources. They have been in control of them since. We spend huge amounts of money in an effort to reacquire those resources.

In the black community, our trends are often determined by the people in the streets such as the hustlers, gangsters, dealers, OG's, and pimps. These people are mentors to a lot of young brothers in the hood. Many brothers credit people from the streets for helping them to be successful. These cats have money, dress well, drive nice cars, wear expensive jewelry, and have many women. Any youngster would desire this life, especially if it's some-body they know. It's difficult for the school to compete with that. Their heroes often have no high school diploma, technical or college degrees.

To a young black man living in poverty, the thug life is enticing. The quest to be like their heroes can come at a cost. You jeopardize your life; you risk getting robbed, assaulted, or arrested. Getting arrested too much leads to a criminal record which has become a scarlet letter. This can be verified by an ex-con. These brothers are subjugated to a different social-economic class, as detailed in **Michele Alexander's** book **"The New Jim Crow."**

I know a man has to survive; who am I or anyone else to judge? Who knows what a man would do if his babies were starving? I've ranted about education throughout this book. I contemplated dropping out of school several times, but education does offer an option.

The failure of education is fundamental. Where are the classes on sex? Maybe if our children are educated about sex, it might prevent many un-wanted pregnancies? Like mental health, this is a topic black people fear to discuss openly. Where are the classes on finance? These classes could teach us how to manage our money better. Every day we spend felicitously on items we don't need. Most of us don't have any concept of saving. We have practically helped to make many companies billions. Where are the classes on the criminal justice system? These classes can educate us on the law to know what to do when confronted by law enforcement. They should be teaching this in our high schools.

It's a tough road for us that causes a tremendous amount of stress. These issues are real to every black man in America regardless of their social or economic class. Some brothers have succeeded despite these obstacles; however, these brothers aren't less affected by racism white supremacy. Some of the brothers in this class endured it even more. These brothers should be commended for their achievements; most of them worked hard to get where they are. Brothers like these should be mentoring in the community. Most brothers work very hard, but some are unwilling. This class of brothers searches for easy ways to make it.

In March of 1991, **"New Jack City"** premiered in theaters. The film was the directorial debut of **Mario Van Peebles. Ice T** makes his acting debut in the movie that also stars **Wesley Snipes, Allen Payne, Bill Nunn, Christopher Williams**, and **Chris Rock**. The film is about a ruthless drug lord named **Nino Brown** and his notorious crew, the **C.M.B.**

Some brothers watched this movie then started emulating Nino Brown just like they did Tony Montana. Acts of violence became brazen and reprehensible. New Jack City was a movie Snipes, and the others were just actors. These scenes are written from a script; recreating them may get you killed or arrested.

The brothers of this class are excellent in math and science. That's why they make a lot of money from successfully manufacturing drugs like chemists.

This is a demonstration of their business acumen. We often hear brothers in this class claim that the game is all they know. I'm not privileged to every black man's experience, but most of the brothers I knew in the game had options. Nobody I knew that hustled was forced into the business like they do people in Mexico or South America. Despite Nino Brown being a snitch and Tony Montana being a junkie, brothers still revere them.

Some of us glorify ignorance then get offended when people disrespect their intelligence. Some rappers started adopting altered egos emulating notorious mob figures reinventing themselves with Italian aliases. Italians resented this and didn't welcome all the unwanted attention. Rappers like 50 Cent, Capone, Noriega, and Rick Ross bear names of legendary Black or Latino gangsters.

We are in a time where there's a wealth of information to assist you in your chosen career. College shouldn't be eliminated as an option. You can get grants or scholarships to help pay for tuition. Getting a job won't hurt either. Our forefathers achieved more despite the hurdles they had to get over. They paved the way showing us all the possibilities.

Some brothers have issues with finding employment because they are unwilling to "work for the white man." They use this excuse as if it's an act of nobility. Since they aren't many black businesses, their sources for employment are limited. Our failure to support black businesses made this all possible. Do you remember we wanted to be integrated? So they disregard any job for this reason then go back to slinging. Some think they are smarter than the previous kingpin; then, they join them in Angola or Rest Haven. How many of these brothers know where the drugs they sell come from?

Through much of the '70s, **George Jung** was a major drug smuggler working for the Medellin cartel. Known as **"Boston George,"** he smuggled thousands of pounds of cocaine into the United States. He was one of the most successful drug smugglers in the United States history. It's been reported an average load he smuggled would net him upwards of 15 million dollars. As I mentioned earlier, the C.I.A placed drugs in black communities helping to finance the Contra's. The Mafia has historically controlled most of the drug trade in America. They supplied drugs to the most powerful drug lords in **New York**, **Boston**, **Chicago**, and **Philadelphia**. "I don't want to work for the white man" is an ignorant statement when the drugs they sell can be purchased, transported, and manufactured by "the white man." They never consider creating their own businesses like the "white man." Some of these brothers eventually end up working for a pittance for white lawyers, judges, sheriffs, and wardens. These officials own some of the prisons they ship them off to.

Prisons are corporations that buy and sell stock on Wall Street; it's a modern-day form of slave trading. Prisoners make a plethora of items; they're no longer just making license plates. This free labor provides huge profits to those that run for-profit prisons similar to the slave owner.

The lure of fast money is attractive; there's nothing like making a few grand a day. Once a brother is initiated into the thug life, he finds it hard to escape. Think about how hard the decision would be to stop slinging only to make 9.00 an hour. Some of these brothers have felony records making it hard for them to find employment.

I'm not so blind that I can't see that wealthy and educated brothers struggle too; however, most of their struggles usually aren't detrimental. There are laws designed for our genocide. Despite that, we must fight to live righteously. Too often, a black man's worth is based on how many women he can conquer or how "gangsta" he is. This ends up in prison time or getting killed, not to mention all the unwanted children. Most of us come from fatherless homes then perpetuate the same cycle as adults.

Irresponsibly the brothers that sell drugs blow a lot of that money. Some of them rain dollars down in various strip clubs. Some brothers participate in various ways to emasculate themselves. Nowadays, it's not uncommon to see some black men dressed in women's attire or wearing makeup. Much of this behavior is because of sexual abuse or incarceration.

In prison, there's a subculture of homosexuality. Some prisoners preyed on weaker inmates, intimidating them then forcing them to perform sexual acts. Some inmates adapt to this lifestyle as a means of protection. In prison, they accept companionship with men, but they resume a heterosexual life- once they are released. This is known as the "down-low," a subculture of men who randomly engage in homosexuality. Except these men don't consider themselves gay. They have discreet liaisons with each other, some-times unprotected. This deviant sexual behavior helped to contribute to the spread of aids in the community. It also brought scrutiny upon brothers. We shouldn't have to prove our masculinity to a sister. The brothers who live this lifestyle are in denial. They should be honest about their sexuality. Being gay has become acceptable; there's no reason to keep this hidden.

I've heard rumors about certain rap artists who may be gay. Some people say they keep their sexuality hidden not to lose their fans or sponsors. Money or endorsements shouldn't matter if you are serious about who you are. I used to listen to some musicians who I suspected were gay. When some eventu-ally came out, it didn't affect how I felt about them. A true fan will support you regardless. We should consider these individual hypocrites considering they are conveniently gay. Homosexuality isn't based on who is the dom-inant partner either. I heard some brothers use this to exclude themselves as gay.

Most of the brothers that hustle never follow the examples of the Italians, Jews, and Irishmen they love to imitate or the clever black drug lords in the movies. We rarely see them start a business that employs people from the communities they exploit. In the '90s, some of them started record labels. They were trying to copy record executives that made the same transition. Most of the brothers that attempted these business ventures weren't really into music, so a lot of wack shit was released.

Some of these companies were only set up for nefarious purposes. The artists they chose to sign were either undeveloped or wack. Due to their shady business dealings, most of these labels only dealt with their core group of artists. There wasn't any attempt to bring in better talent to improve the product. Music was not their main business, so the production often got ignored. Flimsy production and undeveloped artists flooded the market. This blurred the lines between real Hip Hop and the music business. With lots of money available, these labels paid radio executives to get their artist played. Some of these songs received heavy rotation, and since repetition sells, some of them became hits. This came at the expense of well-prepared rappers, DJs, and producers.

In **1972** The murder of **Robert Ballou** was believed to be the specific incident that created a rift among a group of young black men in **Los Angeles**. According to reports, Mr. Ballou was beaten by a group of young men who were attempting to rob him of his leather jacket in a club. This incident is believed to be the event that started gang banging. In retaliation, a splinter group formed, calling themselves the **Bloods**. Since then, the **Crips** and the **Bloods** have grown. Originally known as west coast gangs, they have spread to east coast cities like **New York**, **Washington D.C.**, and **Philadelphia**. It's even been reported that countries like **Holland**, **Paris,** and **Germany** have Blood and Crip sets. How can the murder of one man start such a heinous chain of events? Was Robert Ballou more important than what we know? How come these brothers just didn't have those responsible punished without causing such division? The murders of Medgar Evers, Malcolm X, Fred Hampton, Bobby Hutton, or Martin Luther King didn't cause this kind of reaction.

In the late '80s, tons of reports came out involving innocent victims caught up in the crossfire of gangs. Their victims included innocent children, the disabled, and the elderly. People were beaten or killed because they ventured off into the wrong neighborhood.

Members of gangs fail to see how they have become prisoners in their own communities. All of their actions have caused a self-imposed Martial law. In some gang set's opposing gangs surround them, confining them to specific sections of the city. The insanity of that would drive the average person crazy, yet many gang members have adapted. Some of them teach their children the same behavior, thus repeating the cycle.

We always recruit each other to do foolishness then find ourselves in difficult situations. This shows that some black men can be poor examples. In **1992** rival gangs in **Los Angeles** agreed to a truce under the direction of **NFL Hall Of Famer Jim Brown**. Mr. Brown's efforts towards eradicating gang violence should be applauded. His **Amer-I-Can** organization has successfully turned around the lives of many ex-gang members. Since retiring from the NFL, he has worked diligently to bring attention to the struggles of the inner city. Many gang members present expressed an overwhelming sense of relief. A lot of disputes were resolved, saving an undetermined amount of lives. The truce was short- lived though many of them have resumed their old rivalries.

OG's like **T. Rodgers**, **Michael Concepcion,** and **Larry Hoover** frown upon these acts. All these brothers have created positive programs to help steer gang members away from that life. Most gang members have no idea why they hate each other or the core principles of their gang members. I won't cast any of the founders as boy scouts; most of them will tell you this themselves. They were brothers in the streets, but they understood a "code of the streets" that cannot be violated. They had by-laws established that added structure to the gang. These by-laws helped to keep them from attracting unwanted attention from law enforcement. They were instrumental in helping to filter out disingenuous members. The acts committed by some gang members today wouldn't be allowed under their leadership.

"They might say we're a menace to society, But at the same time I say "Why is it me?" Am I the target for destruction? What about the system, and total corruption?

Gangstarr "Code Of The Streets"

Larry Hoover, the founding chairman of the **Gangsta Disciples,** has worked hard to change the gang he helped establish. He changed the direction of the Gangster Disciples focusing the group on **Growth** and **Development**. He urged his members to get out and vote, including ex-felons. **Stanley "Tookie" Williams**, the co-founder of the Crips, went to his grave, urging gang members to end the bloodshed. While in prison, he authored books on gangs in an effort to bring awareness.

How many kingpins finance positive programs? White people love drugs as much as we do, maybe more. How come the trappers aren't brave enough to set up shop in a white neighborhood? They certainly have in ours.

Is a lot of our behavior due to a lack of having fathers in our lives? Issues surrounding black fatherhood have roots in slavery. The black home was constantly broken up. Slaves were bought and sold frequently then sent to other plantations. Slave fathers and mothers were disconnected from their children, so mentally, they learned to adapt. Some slave men were used primarily as studs specifically selected to procreate. They were never allowed to have an emotional attachment to the children they produced or the mother. That mentality was passed on through the generations creating a pattern.

No one should be so decorated to suggest black men don't care for their children. We love our children as much as any other group of men, but relationships with our children is sometimes a complex maze. That includes the courts and the women we choose to impregnate. Some of us are unwise about selecting a partner. Too many of us overlook obvious inequities in the women we choose. Then we blame them instead of ourselves. Men are supposed to be rational thinkers devoid of emotion when making intelligent decisions. The list of bad decisions we make concerning women could fill this chapter.

Most black men in America were raised in a matriarchal environment. This is why some of us are more emotional than men of other ethnicities. This causes a need to exert a lot of testosterone. The matriarchal structure makes us very protective of women. Our love for the black woman and disdain for the black man (ourselves) keep us blind to many of their shortcomings.

With more than 22 million black women in this country, some brothers would kill each other over scandalous women. They never evaluate this situation which often ends in one brother dead and the other locked up—leaving that sister to get with another guy.

Some educated or wealthy brothers are the worst ones among us. These types of brothers are also the most dangerous. This class of brothers understands us well; many of them came from the community. They have a great understanding of our strengths and weaknesses. They use this information mostly to enrich themselves. Much like the brother who hustles, he has many material possessions and an unlimited choice in women. Some of these brothers boasted that it is their educational achievements that make them superior. I won't suggest to any brother not to be proud of their accomplishments, but when you use them to be condescending, there is when you will know you have crossed the line. Most of these brothers benefitted from the people in the community, yet they do nothing to improve it. Some rarely become mentors like the ones that helped to make them successful. They become policemen, politicians, judges, social workers, educators, and clergy members, etc., then move far away. To gain acceptance, they join up with groups of white people. Some join covert groups in an attempt to differentiate themselves from the rest of us. This is how the brothers of this class cope with being a black man in America.

An example of this type of brother is in the movie **"The Drop Squad,"** starring **Eric LaSalle**, **Vondie Curtis Hall,** and **Ving Rhames**. The Drop Squad was about a pro-black group that kidnapped missguided black people. They take them to a secret location then deprogram them of their self-hatred. The main character is a brother named Bruford Jamison. He is a marketing executive who has no problem creating advertisements that reinforce stereotypes. This included a vulgar campaign his firm created for a beer company promoting malt liquor. In his quest to succeed in the company, he betrays his co-workers then turns his back on his family.

Another brother like this can be seen in Spike Lee's **"Bamboozled."** **Damon Wayans** portrays Pierre Delacroix, whose actual name is Peerless Dothan. Dothan is a Harvard-educated brother who works for CNS, a fictional television station in New York. He's disgusted with his job and his boss Thomas Dunwitty constantly rejects his scripts. He writes positive black programs that he feels are being unfairly denied. In retaliation, he composed a minstrel show, and he intended for Mr. Dunwitty to hate the script so much that he would fire him. This would release him from his contract freeing him up to other opportunities. Surprisingly Dunwitty loves the idea then gives him the go-ahead to start production. This placed him in an awkward position to produce the show. On the advice of his assistant Sloan Hopkins, he recruits two talented homeless brothers to star in the show named Man Ray and Womack. At first, they have reservations about the show after it's revealed they would be required to mask in blackface. They also had a problem acting out the degrading content in the script. After more reassurance by Delacroix, they agreed to star in the show billed as **"Man Tan The New Millennium Minstrel Show."** The show instantly becomes a hit then he begins to bask in his success. His original intentions are abandoned. When criticism comes from the public surrounding the offensive content, he defends the show content calling it "satirical."

These two scenarios describe the situations some educated brothers can find themselves in. They are left to choose between money and loyalty. Some brothers go into politics, business, theology, and law enforcement with good intentions but get fascinated by power and money. Once they approve of these temptations, they abandon their cause becoming agents of the same system.

January 20, 2009, Barack Hussein Obama is sworn in as the **44th President** of the **United States**. This historical event was perceived to be the culmination of all the sacrifices of our forefathers. The black community celebrated President Obama's arrival. Obama being elected was seen as a monumental achievement demonstrating the heights that a black man could achieve. The charismatic president brought a sense of pride to black people worldwide. Some black people saw President Obama as a prophet or a messiah. Some of us naively thought decades of racism would be eradicated, but actually, it got worse. President Obama endured unprecedented disrespect for a seated president, including being called a monkey, antisemitic, and questionable citizenship. South Carolina Senator Joe Wilson accused him of being a liar as he addressed the nation from the senate floor.

Some in the black community scolded him for not addressing issues of race. It's unreasonable to suggest that he could have reversed decades of racism. Some blacks look at his interracial parents as an example of his disconnect from the average black man. Time will tell the impact of President Obama and how much he benefited the black community.

President Obama's father being **African** conjures up some harbored feelings blacks in the United States share. Some of us felt abandoned by the brothers from the continent. Many questions why weren't Africans instrumental in helping to end slavery or Jim Crow? Some African tribe leaders' participation in the slave trade fuels much of the division.

Black Americans traveled to Africa, exposing our mistreatment in America. **July 21, 1964, Malcolm X** spoke at the **2nd annual OAU**. At the conference, he made African leaders aware of our experiences. Most of them did nothing, nor did they speak out against it. They seemed not to care about the US policy involving their captured brothers. A few African leaders visited the US during these times but ignored what they witnessed.

Blacks born in America supported their African brothers during their struggles to end apartheid. African American political leaders, clergy members, actors, and musicians contributed a lot of money and time. This kind of pressure led to the end of apartheid.

Some Africans travel to the United States to earn college degrees. Most of them come here and take the same attitudes towards us as oppressors. We must develop better relationships with our brothers in Africa. We deal with the same devil just on different continents. If we engage collectively, we can solve a lot of our problems.

Some of us place a huge amount of trust in the political system. I understand that politics govern all the aspects surrounding the quality of our lives. A taxpayer has the same power as the voter, but the voter is more likely to be heard. We are advised to vote regularly, but the limited amount of qualified candidates make voting a gamble. Many of us avoid the political process after witnessing years of corruption. We have an excessive amount of political figures that seek to further their own agenda. They blatantly overlook the interest of the people that elected them while conspiring with our open enemies. When there are many undesirable candidates, we are recommended to vote for "the lesser of evil," but why should we be forced to vote for anyone evil?

It would be unfair to expect any political candidate to be free of all transgressions. This may be humanly impossible; however, they must not be guilty of violating the law or the public trust. Some blacks feel insulted by the notion of a black person not voting. They cite the struggles our people endured while fighting for this civil right. The struggles of our forefathers should never be ignored; we should always honor our people. We have fought for plenty of other stuff that we neglect more. Some of us see political corruption then decide they want no part of that bureaucracy. Informing voters and genuine politicians could bring changes in this area. We should form our own political party then aggressively seek candidates that will serve the community's best interest.

It's **1989,** my time at Fortier will be ending soon. I will be leaving this coolass school. You might have noticed I referred to my alma mater as being "cool." On several occasions when I say that, I'm referring to the student body, the athletic programs, the band, the school newspaper, and some of the teachers; however, the academics weren't "cool" at all. No history class taught us anything significant about our people. Like my previous schools, we were taught a heavy doctrine of European ideology. Distributive education, chemistry, and mathematics are the only subjects that attempted to prepare us for the future.

I decided to enlist in the Navy. I schedule myself to leave a week after graduation. I had to leave New Orleans to find out what life was all about. I was fed up hoping to connect with like-minded people, and a **brother was gonna work it out**.

In June, I arrived at boot camp, which ended up being more of a challenge than I thought. Every day I was tested mentally and physically. I didn't think I would miss my mama or home that much. I found out immediately that New Orleans had the best food in the world. I was in San Diego, California; this place was like a different world to me. I was on my own, starting the process of becoming a man. I met some great brothers from all over the United States. I learned that we all share the same struggles. A couple of months later, I was sent to a fire fighting school on Treasure Island San Francisco.

In **1990 Public Enemy** released **"Fear Of A Black Planet" Professor Griff** still hadn't rejoined the group. I was disappointed, but without him, P.E. continued on. The same year Professor Griff released **"Pawns In The Game"** on **Luke Records**. **Ice Cube** survived the negativity surrounding him departing **NWA**. He formed his own squad of west coast rappers called **"Da Lench Mob."** In **1990** he released **"Kill At Will** and **"Amerikkkas Most Wanted."** He connected with legendary producers **The Bomb Squad** that consisted of **Chuck D, Eric Sadler, Hank Shocklee,** and **Keith Shocklee.** This collaboration worked well and took both parties to another level opening them up to a different audience.

In **1991 NWA** follow-up album **"Niggaz 4 Life"** was released to huge commercial success. The departure of Ice Cube didn't affect their movement. Ice Cube's non-fatal departure should have been a motto for many in rap music to embrace. Since then, many rap artists have chosen to handle these situations differently. This has resulted in a lot of violence and diss recordings.

Too often, we look at violence as a means of handling disputes. There's little to no effort to resolve the conflict. The Italians, some brothers imitated, knew the value of conflict resolution. Members of the Mafia have ended heated conflicts that negatively affected their business. Respect is so important to some black men that they would kill each other over it. Arab, Asian and white-owned businesses disrespect them daily in the hood, but they do nothing.

In **1990** a cadre of conscious MCs dropped albums. **X Clan** released **"To The East Black Wards."** X Clan was an extremely conscious rap group out of **Brooklyn**. The group consisted of the **"The Grand Verbalizer" Brother**

J, **Professor X "The Overseer"**, **Paradise,** and **DJ Suga Shaft**. They carried staffs wore Afrocentric garbs, beads, and big black boots. They did rap songs about Egypt filling in the blinks left out by the school. They were affiliated with an organization called the **"Black Watch"** which exposed us to more of their activism.

Out of **Now Rule (New Rochelle, NY)** came the **Brand Nubians** with their debut album **"One For All."** **The Brand Nubians** consisted of **Grand Puba, Lord Jamar, Sadat X,** and **DJ Alamo**. Their **Five Percenter** infused lyrics brought an unprecedented amount of consciousness to Hip Hop; this makes their album among the years' most critically acclaimed. The album should have been platinum, but mostly all of the sales of this album were from bootleggers. How come a group this important had to endure having their music stolen? The Brand Nubians should have been rewarded for their work on this classic album.

The **Poor Righteous Teachers** were from **New Jerusalem (New Jersey);** the group featured **Wise Intelligent, Culture Freedom,** and **Dj Father Shaheed**. Their debut album **"Holy Intellect"** exhibited an impressive level of consciousness. **The Gods** showcased a distinctive style of rap they called the **"Butt Naked Booty Bless."** This group was one of the standard barriers of the conscious rap movement. Out of the Bay area came **Paris's** debut album, **"The Devil Made Me Do It."** This was a scorching piece that gave Hip Hop a purely conscious MC out of the west coast. Labeled **"The Black Panther Of Rap,"** his Panther influenced lyrics were politically educational and empowering. He represented well coming from the area where the Panthers were founded.

Slick Rick was arrested after shooting his cousin, leading the police on a high- speed car chase. He was convicted of attempted murder then sentenced to 5 years. Slick Rick becomes the first high profile rapper to do time. This taught us the stardom of Hip Hop might not exclude you from the drama of the streets.

A Tribe Called Quest released their debut album "People's Instinctive Travels And The Paths Of Rhythm" this album gave rap music a fresh sound. Out of Queens, the group featured Qtip, Phife Dawg, Dj Ali Shaheed, and Jarobi. This album laid the foundation for them to become one of the most creative rap groups in the history of Hip Hop. ATCQ was part of The Native Tongues Hip Hop collective featuring Queen Latifah,DeLaSoul, The Jungle Brothers, Black Sheep, Chi Ali, The Fu-Schnickens and outta London Monie Love.

The Fresh Prince (Will Smith) becomes the first rap artist to star on a television show. "The Fresh Prince Of Bel-Air" was a hit offering a flattering look of the black family on network television. His performance on television would lead to greater success as an actor.

Oakland remained relevant after MC Hammer released his multi-platinum album "Please Hammer Don't Hurt Em." Dancing is a huge part of Hip Hop Hammer takes it to another level creating new dance moves that become a staple. His dance-infused music was reminiscent of the days when party songs were normal in rap music.

The importance of dance has always been a high priority among the culture. Even during the days of the big band era, some songs made everyone want to dance. The dances that were historically connected to Hip Hop originated in the Bronx. The moves they invented were very physical and rhythmic. They displayed these moves mostly on the breakbeats that the DJs would spin. They became known as break-dancers. This improvisational style of the dance showed a high level of energy and creativity.

MC Hammer endured a lot of criticism from so-called "real" Hip Hop heads. Most of them were accusing him of dumbing down the content. I'm sure some of the criticism was fueled by jealousy. There was still a lot of diversity in rap during this time, so no rapper should have been targeted.

Most of his critics were other disgruntled rappers because the people liked him. He was selling many albums and filling up a lot of arenas. Some people didn't recognize his generosity; he employed many people from the community he was raised in. MC Hammer should have been applauded for that instead of labeled a "sellout."

Another talented group emerged out of Oakland named **Digital Underground**. Their debut release, **"Sex Packets,"** quickly catches on nationwide. Their hit singles **"Do What You Like"** and **"The Humpty Dance"** would have many people rushing to the dance floor. The funk genius of **Shock G** shines as he switches in and out of his alter ego **Humpty Hump**. Unbeknownst to us at the time, D.U. introduced us to a young **Tupac Shakur**

LL Cool J released arguably his greatest album, **"Mama Said Knock You Out."** He enlisted the help of legendary **Juice Crew** producer **Marly Marl**. Multiple hit songs came from this platinum-selling album, including the title track **"Round The Way Girl," "The Booming System,"** and a successful remix of **"Jingling."** The most interesting song was **"To The Break Of Dawn"** a scathing diss of **Ice T**, **MC Hammer,** and **Kool Moe Dee**. This song had been highly anticipated. Moe Dee and LL had some beef cooking for a while. Kool Moe Dee made references to LL on his hit record **"How You Like Me Now" "I'm bigger and better forget about deffer."** His album cover had a photo of his Suzuki jeep rolling over LL's signature Kangol hat. Ice T has taken his fair share of jabs at LL. On his underground classic **"Dog'n The Wax,"** he says, **"the player from L.A. cooler than any J my name is Ice T. I make the Mafia pay." "Dog'n The Wax"** Ice T. On **"Power,"** he dissed him again on **"I'm Your Pusher"** and once more on **"The Syndicate."**

Hammer took shots at **LL Cool J, Doug E Fresh,** and **Run DMC**. Most of us felt like they brought this upon themselves. The criticism of LL Cool

J was unwarranted. From afar, it looked like jealousy played a part in these skirmishes. Kool Moe Dee seemed upset that old school MCs weren't given proper recognition. He's quoted as saying his reason for dissing LL was hearing him declare himself **"the greatest rapper in the history of rap itself" "I'm Bad" LL Cool J**. With all the boasting that goes on in rap, why single out one line in someone's song?

LL Cool J never appeared as the aggressor cleverly; he made them look like the villains. These rap battles remained confined to wax. Some of the rap battles have resulted in disputes that sometimes ended in the loss of lives. Incidents like these give the media ammunition to cast negative aspersions on rap artists. I know some jazz, rock, country, pop, and R&B artists have disagreements, but I never heard of them resolving them in this manner.

Some brothers spend so much time trying to "keep it real," which sometimes means real ignorant, real disrespectful, or really distasteful. Nowadays, some brothers wear their trousers low, exposing their undergarments. This fashion trend started in the penile system. Two stories exist on why they dressed that way. Both stories are credible; multiple ex-convicts revealed them to me. The first reason they cite is that some prisons required inmates to remove their belts to deter them from using them as a weapon or for suicide. The other reason is that certain inmates wore their pants low to show they were available to be taken as sex partners. When these inmates were released, some continue to dress this way after years of being accustomed. Many black kids adopted this fashion trend imitating how these brothers dressed. After rappers started dressing that way, it became popular. It's now an eyesore to most of us in the community.

Some brothers get released from prison then make something out of their lives. These brothers are a divine testament to the community, but far too many come out portraying prison like a summer camp or a rite of passage. You should hear how they proudly tell their prison stories. With all the boasting, where are the tales of the murders, rapes, extortions, and the abuse by crooked correctional officers? These are the stories that might deter young brothers from prison, maybe saving their lives. The reality never sets in for this class of brothers until they are faced with multiple years in prison. Since prisons are for profit, there are few stories of redemption. Most prisons have eliminated opportunities for felons to continue their education or learn a trade.

Let's look at the black athletes, actors, and musicians. Most of these brothers praise the matriarchs in their families. On draft night, they parade their mothers around in expensive shoes, gowns, and jewelry. After scoring a touchdown, if a camera is present, they always yell "hi ma!" When accepting awards for their accomplishments, they always praise their mothers and grandmothers, and then most of them go out and marry white women. With all that black women mean to these brothers, you would certainly think they would be honored to marry one. Various reasons exist why this happens so much to brothers in this class.

Many brothers in this class claim black women are gold diggers, disrespectful, untrustworthy, and some even say unattractive. The same can be said of white women; however, the white girl gets the benefit of the doubt. I'm not trying to determine who someone should marry, but this is more of the norm among these brothers. It's baffling that brothers in this class cannot find good black women with the same values as the matriarchs they praise. This should be impossible considering all the black women available to them. Some of these brothers have children with sisters, but they still chose to marry the white girl. The value of black women is reduced to a sexual object. The same thing that happened to the matriarchs' lives in their families by the men is repeated by them.

I'm not the first one to shine a light on black men. **The Honorable Elijah Muhammad's "Message To The Black Man," Hakim Madhubuti's**

"BlackMen, Obsolete, Single or Dangerous," Andre Akil "From Nigga's To Gods" and Michael Porter "Kill Them Before They Grow" are books that tell similar stories. We have to shed the differences between us and embrace our similarities. There are people in high parts of the government with agendas towards our demise. The school system will not be solely responsible for properly educating our babies. We need to commit to making better choices than start serving as beacons to our communities. Black men take a careful look at things that may endanger your life or risk your freedom. We need to stop this cycle to be around for our families.

By the end of the summer of **1990,** the hottest rap song was **"Ice Ice Baby" by Vanilla Ice,** a white boy from **Dallas, Texas.** The song steals a well-known chant from **Alpha Phi Alpha,** a black fraternity. Like always, here comes the great white hope hijacking our ideas. We had no problem with him being white because we had white rappers; he just didn't seem authentic. His debut album **"To The Extreme" went** multi-platinum dealing a serious blow to what conscious rap artists were building.

I guess these white executives weren't going to keep allowing **Paris** to expose the misdeeds of their ancestors in songs like **"Break The Grip Of Shame." "Why Is That" Krs-One** had to confirm that the people of the bible were indeed black? They didn't want us to **"Heed The Word Of The Brother."** The powers that be rather we not listen to **The Black Watch. Brand Nubians** urging sisters to **"Slow Down"** wasn't selling enough records. They preferred we had amoral scantily dressed sisters running around. They were afraid to answer **Public Enemy's** question, **"Who Stole The Soul?"** because the answer would expose them. Nope, the industry wanted us to tone that black shit down and dance. Ice, Ice Baby history has a strange way of repeating itself. **It's not a conspiracy it's a plan.** That's ok cause....

"As you raise your fist to the music. United we stand divided, we fall together we can stand tall." "Brothers Gonna Work It Out" Public Enemy.

CHAPTER 8

KEEP YA HEAD UP

"Some say the blacker the berry, the sweeter the juice. I say the darker the flesh then the deeper the roots. I give a holla to my sisters on welfare Tupac cares, if don't nobody else cares." "Keep Ya Head Up" Tupac Shakur.

The black woman is the most beautiful creation on this planet. There's no woman more beautiful than her. World-wide black women's features are copied. Women of other races endure painful surgeries or risk radiation poisoning trying to emulate her. The personification of wisdom she's comparable to the Earth. Like the planet, she gives and receives life. She's universally desired; she comes in different shades, shapes, and sizes. **Wu-Tang** said it best **"French vanilla, butter pecan, chocolate deluxe even caramel sundaes are getting touched and scooped in my ice cream truck Wu tears it up" "Ice Cream" Wu-TangClan.** Her curves are like the **Nile** making brothers want to drink from her fountain. She understands the black man better than any woman on this planet. Through all our struggles, she has stood by our side.

Black women like **Harriet Tubman**, **Sojourner Truth**, **Frances Cress Welsing**, **Coretta Scott King,** and **Betty Shabazz** were loyal, courageous, dedicated, and virtuous. They demonstrated good character setting great examples for all women to follow.

Sisters struggle daily, raising our children mostly alone. It's remarkable how the black woman consistently keeps the family going. They bravely take on roles they are unprepared for excelling despite the odds. Like I mentioned earlier, sometimes I never knew how my mama made ends meet. Every black mother should be commended for her amazing achievements, especially if she's doing it alone.

Back in chattel slavery, the black woman raised her children and slave masters. This showed that our women had a tremendous ability to nurture. In the movie Gone With The Wind, **Hattie McDaniel Oscar** winning role as "Mammy" was considered demeaning, but actually, she was the rock of that family. She played an important role in the lives of the people she worked for, just like the black women who worked as domestics. These sisters showed a tremendous amount of discipline, enduring unfathomable abuse to feed their families.

During those times, the black family was connected, two-parent homes were normal, and everyone accepted their roles. When chronicling the events that started discord in our families, we must go back to the late '60s. Fed up with being mistreated by white men, caucasian women started the feminist movement. White women were pissed off with the roles they played in their families. They demanded an end to domestic violence, the right to work outside the home, equal pay, maternity leave, control over reproduction, and the end to sexual harassment. These things had been happening to them for a long time, and they were no longer going to accept it. For years they tried to address these issues but were always met with strong opposition.

In **1969 Gloria Stenium** published an article titled **"After Black Power, Women's Liberation."** The obvious move was to use the momentum of the civil rights movement to push a feminist agenda. This would help white women attain their goal of equality while weakening the gains of the civil rights movement.

Margaret Sanger had been financing research on birth control for years to develop a pill to control reproduction. Mrs. Sanger was a wealthy woman who was a member of the Sanger family world-renowned for their sewing machines. She was a eugenicist determined to find a way to control reproduction. Since **1916** she opened up unsanitary birth control clinics that authorities would immediately close. A lot of women died from infections while undergoing those procedures. These clinics were the first Planned Parenthood Centers.

In **1917** the United States introduced **Operation Bootstrap** in **Puerto Rico**. This program was supposedly designed to improve the economy of the Island. In a plan to control the birth rate on the island, scientists started secret birth control experiments on the women. They allegedly did these experiments out of concern that the workforce would be affected negatively. Puerto Rican women that worked in these factories were getting pregnant, hurting production. The U.S. government thought the Puerto Ricans were unable to make intelligent decisions on reproduction. As a result of these covert experiments, over **1/3** of the women involved were sterilized. Once again, the USA uses a group of impoverished people as guinea pigs.

In the late **60's** pharmaceutical companies improved on this research then started marketing the birth control pill. The reason behind developing the pill was as a means of population control along with abortion. The people involved in making this pill were eugenics with racist intentions. I understand these days that condoms are used for more than birth control. The current rate of sexually transmitted diseases makes condoms a requirement. I just wanted to educate sisters on the history of birth control and its relation to the feminist movement.

It wasn't uncommon for black families to be large. My great grandfather had **12** children. He worked hard, and his family was well taken care of. Many of his children went on to finish college or had successful careers. This shatters the myth by Europeans that these children go neglected. My family story is not unique; there are plenty of others similar. The leaders of the feminist movement knew for their demands to be taken seriously, they needed to recruit help. So they sought out naive black women to join their movement. Black women bought credibility along with the ability to organize. Many sisters learned these skills while working in the civil rights movement. It was a successful tactic; eventually, many of their demands were met. Laws were passed barring gender discrimination intended on improving behavior in the workplace. Companies then began to hire more women to satisfy government requirements. **Title nine** was passed in **1972,** barring discrimination based on sex. This meant any schools receiving federal money would have to allow women to compete for scholarships, money for social programs, and athletics.

It's the early **70s,** not even ten years removed from the signing of the civil rights act. Sisters had fought with black men collectively; now, some wanted to be liberated. If black women were being mistreated, where was the black women's movement? **Angela Davis, Bell Hooks,** and **Patricia Hill Collins** certainly were present. When were black women so abused by black men considering all of us were catching hell? How did this become our issue?

In **1965 President Lyndon B. Johnson** signed into law **executive order 11246,** commonly known as **affirmative action.** This law required that no company in America can hire without regard to race, religion, or natural origin. Many black women were hired; by doing this, companies satisfied two government-friendly requirements hiring a black person and a woman. The white man found a clever way to use these laws. This resulted in many white women being shut out of the workforce after all. Unfortunately, some of these jobs had been previously held by black men. Brothers were starting to be shut out of the workforce.

With the black woman as the primary breadwinner, the roles in the family became reversed. The power structure of the black family shifted. Systematically the black family was starting to be divided. A lot of brothers left their families frustrated because they were unable to provide for them. Some brothers resulted in crime as a way to provide for their families. This started the cycle of incarceration. Some brothers tried to cope by using illegal drugs, prescription medication, and alcohol. The abuse the feminist movement was supposed to stop actually started. Black women were left abandoned, ushering in single-parent homes.

Once the men they loved departed, issues of self-esteem started overwhelming them. Some ended up in a cycle of temporary relationships that often bought on more children. The baby mama/daddy era had begun, I find them to be demeaning. I never liked those terms; they are often used when referring to unwed black parents. The terms suggest that the father is a dead beat or the mother is unfit. Those that use these terms should think about this. According to the bible, **God** is the father of **Jesus,** born through Mary's womb. This would make God Mary's "baby daddy." She was married to **Joseph** to make God and Mary guilty of adultery. Some would call this blasphemous, but when you consider the context in which that term is used, it fits exactly.

Many black women became hardened after years of not having a man around. Most of them concluded that they "didn't need a man." So that meant their children's fathers were no longer needed in their lives. Some learn how to use the courts and the welfare system to gain income. Some sisters took the money ordered to them by the courts for the children and spent it lavishly on themselves. They quit working and stayed home entertaining themselves by watching soap operas.

"I don't think I can handle she goes channel to channel, cold looking for that hero, she watches channel zero." "Channel Zero" Public Enemy.

The soap opera was the equivalent of the housewives' reality shows we see today. As they sat around watching these soaps, they began to fantasize about the lives of the characters they followed. This caused them to have unreasonable expectations of brothers. The average brother doesn't have the means to lavish gifts like they do in the soaps. They offered brothers nothing in return like the actresses they follow.

Their desire to look like these women had become evident. Sales of products like Nadinola shot up as black women started bleaching their skin. Their afros were replaced with wigs, weaves, and perms.

Many sisters stayed in school and earned degrees. Some of them did well enough to move up in corporate America. Some started to date men of other races, while some started to date other women. Many women developed bad attitudes that were passed on to their daughters. Men's movement groups singled out bad attitudes among their chief complaints of black women, but where did these attitudes come from? Is it from rejection by the men in their lives? Is it from abuse or a trained, learned behavior? All of the above can be listed as factors. Sexual abuse was overlooked in this country until revelations of sexual abuse started coming forth at the end of the 20th century. This issue remained dormant in America. For years the Catholic Church was complicit in allowing scores of young men to be abused by members of their Parishes. This atrocity proved how sexual abuse was hidden inside America and religion under the belly.

Any topic that deals openly with sex is an unpleasant subject for us. We never teach our young girls or young men what to do if an adult does something inappropriate to them. The absence of the black father plays a vital role in a young sister's life. Her father is the first man she can identify with; therefore, she feels abandoned by the most important man in her life. Her mother is the first one she looks to as a mentor; she's the example of black womanhood many of her attributes are instilled within her. This is the foundation of who she is rather her mother has good or bad morals. Some sisters never carefully analyzed this.

Black women took on independence for different reasons than white women. It was a rallying cry; most of them were trying to mask the hurt of being abandoned. Being alone is not normal; there's someone for everyone; however, sisters must be careful of their relationships. Being selective of your partner can be beneficial to your life. Let's evaluate how black women find the men in their lives. When a sister meets a brother, she has all the leverage. She decides who she goes out with, and most sisters aren't so bold as to step to a brother. Most sisters' standards are set according to the men in their lives. Her father, brothers, uncles, or grandfathers often become a representation of all men. The attributes of these men determine the type of men she may have in her private life. The characters of these men play a role in how she would deal with the opposite sex. Brothers that don't measure up to those standards are often rejected. The attributes of the men aforementioned attract them to men of that type. They have been trained to accept those types of men from the matriarchs of their families. So they end up with men in their lives like the ones they were taught to despise. Psychologically, there's an interesting paradigm behind this. If black women have bad men, it's because they allow them into their lives. Sisters select the men they have sex with, date, or marry. Historically a lot of sisters have selected the wrong men. Often the man is blamed for ignoring any self-responsibility.

Some sisters use abortion to control birth; they abort children due to having sex irresponsibly. This is disturbing, considering the black community boasts one of the highest rates of abortion. Plus, black folks are very evangelical abortion don't fit in with that ideology. Many sisters get these procedures done without the father's awareness or consent. The black woman holds tremendous power and can determine life or death.

Black women were bestowed as the "backbone of the family." The black man was demonized, causing relationships between the two to be strained, thereby creating a disconnection between black men and their children. This was all to the glee of our open enemies. As the newly independent black woman took shape, gangs, teenage pregnancy, high school dropout, and teenage delinquency increased.

Some brothers weren't allowed to see their children because some sisters used them as weapons against them. Some brothers tried to remain in their children's lives but had to overcome the hurdle of disgruntled mothers. Some sisters use the courts to keep their children away from their fathers. To the fathers, the constant maze of the legal system was unwavering, unfair, immoral, and expensive. They even conjure up phony cases of abuse or file fallacious protection orders. All of this is done to keep brothers away from their children. Instead of accepting blame for the state of our children, the black man was held responsible. In the last part of the 20th century, a lot of sisters haven't done a good job raising the babies. Do we think these sisters weren't aware of the brothers' character they had children for? Some sisters get with brothers then try to change them. Sometimes it works, but too often, it's unsuccessful. This can come at a price, especially when children are involved.

When converting, their Afros sisters started using perms. Prolonged usage of these dangerous chemicals resulted in chemical burns and hair loss. The demand for wigs and artificial hair got greater among black women. **Madame C.J. Walker** was the first female self-made millionaire in America. She developed a line of hair care and beauty products that she sold worldwide. This industry is controlled by Asians now, as detailed in the **Chris Rock** documentary **"Good Hair."** The black hair care industry started with a black woman; now, the Asians are in control. To most black women, hair is essential; sisters feel like it's a major determinant of how they feel about themselves. They watch white women on television for years, envious of the texture of their hair. The term "good hair" is another self-demeaning analogy demonstrating a lot of self-hatred. The slave masters intermingling with black women caused that group of people to have a different texture of hair. This hair texture was called "good" hair by black people because it mimics that of White's, Latinos or Native American's. They consider "bad hair" to be the unmanageable kinky hair native to our people from Africa. Good hair isn't based on hair texture; it's based on how well you take care of your hair. Those that used these terms never consider how ignorant they sound.

In **Spike Lee's** movie **"School Daze,"** the divide between the two was played out in a scene between the "Jigaboo's" and the "wannabes." Some sisters dye their hair to replicate the colors of European women. Some of them even wear contact lenses to imitate the color of their eyes. After a while, the brothers started going for the white girl instead of the imitation offered to them.

European women became the standard of beauty which made the cosmetic industry rich. I know some sisters will counter claiming women of other nationalities buy cosmetics too; however, the hair care products generate much of the income in this industry. Some sisters go through the extremes to get a hairstyle like a Latino, Asian, or Caucasian woman wears naturally. Mentally blinded, they declare themselves "real women" it's a huge hypocrisy. It's inexplicable, considering white women get butt injections, botox, and tans to look like black women. This shows the need for counseling for our people. We really need a psychological evaluation.

In **Alice Walker's** critically acclaimed novel **"The Color Purple,"** the disdain of the black man is evident. The novel later became an **Oscar-winning** movie directed by **Stephen Spielberg**. The movie featured an all-star cast including **Whoopi Goldberg, Oprah Winfrey, Danny Glover, Adolph Caesar, Rae Dawn Chong,** and **Laurence Fishburn**. The story follows the life of fictional character Celie who has two children by her paedophile father. He gives her away to another older abusive gentleman named Mister. This brother is so disrespectful that he allowed his mistress Suge

Avery to live in the home they shared. He has a son named Harpo, married to a dominant sister named Sophia. Harpo asks Celie for advice on how to handle her. She advises him to beat her, which leads to Sophia and his children leaving him. Celie eventually musters up the strength to leave the abusive Mister. As a show of good faith, he goes out of his way to re- connect Celie with her sister Nettie. Nettie took Celie's children to Africa, where they were raised. Everyone is reunited, and they all lived happily ever after as they played patty cake in the field.

Let's examine all the men in this story. Celie's father was a child molester who conveniently died while having sex with a woman half his age. Her arranged husband, Mister, was an abusive serial philanderer. Harpo was a weak brother who inherited his father's abusive ways. Old Mister Johnson took solace in Celie, but she spits in his drink after scolding Mister to allow Suge Avery to live in their home. I'm not going to say they aren't any black men like this but sisters took this movie as the gospel.

Some sisters are attracted to abusive men; they go through cycles of men like this. Sisters in this class sometimes find non-abusive men then leave them for another abusive one. Some sisters follow some badass advice without considering the source. A sister without a man shouldn't be giving you advice on how to be dealing with yours. These sisters represent a sense of narcism needing justification for their erroneous actions. The worst aspect is that their bitter girlfriend usually pacifies that urge. Some sisters are married that can give better advice, but they bypass them.

It's been estimated **70%** of available black women in America are single. I'm not one to readily accept any statistics related to us; however, I find these numbers accurate. Any black person only has to consider the women in their families or their community to verify this. I know some couples have been together for years regardless of a document stating they married. These statistics may not account for that small percentage of blackwomen. With all that considered, why is this number so high? Are that many black women undesirable? If this isn't true, then why aren't they getting married? Black women have excelled educationally, politically, and financially but they can't find a desirable mate. Brothers are certainly getting married; apparently, they aren't marrying many sisters.

In the previous chapter, I mention brothers on the "down low." Now I will talk about the women who fall for them. Some women are attracted to "bad boys" even some educated women love a gangster. The excitement of these types of relationships is a rush. The rewards are plenty when you consider all the disposable income these cats have. It's easy for a woman to fall for a man that financially takes care of her. Some sisters admire brothers that "get it how they live" unafraid to take a risk. They look the other way as long as it continues to benefit them. When the heat comes like it occasionally does on brothers like this, these women abandon them then find another brother similar. This shows that they also become addicted to that life. Most of these sisters have no desire to marry any of these brothers, nor do they desire to be married. Some find themselves incarcerated mixed up in their boyfriends' criminal activities or dead. Some of these men often go to prison where they live as a homosexual. They eventually get released to dozens of adoring women. This is one of the ways how HIV was passed around the community.

With so many women surrounding these "doughboys," this causes conflicts. I urge you to go to YouTube or WorldstarHipHop and see how many fights they have behind men like this. Some sisters enter into a relationship with men who have multiple children and "baby mamas" only to become another one of them. Common sense should tell them this man doesn't care about the women and children he already has. They are naive in dealing with men like that.

Some sisters can be disingenuous when dealing with each other. Envy encompasses them. You can see this on TV shows like Maury Povich or Paternity Court when they go on there to take DNA tests to identify the fathers of their children. The child's mother and the new girlfriend are always at odds.

Some sisters need to be "independent" until they get their act together. This class of sisters cannot go without a man; they parade different men in and out of their lives. These classes of black women cling onto some worthless-ass brothers. Some of them forsake their children to please these types of men.

Ignoring the mental health of black women has caused problems. Some sisters turned to self-medicating using illegal drugs, alcohol, and prescription medications. In the eighties, some children were born to mothers addicted to crack cocaine. These children were coined "crack babies" then studied in their development. Some of these children grew up with a host of developmental problems. Most of them were diagnosed with ADHD, prescribed mind-altering medication then placed in special education classes. Some were declared disable then placed on social security. Some sisters allowed shady social workers, school administrators, and doctors to misdiagnose their children with ADHD, thereby placing their children on mind-altering drugs. Having prescribed these drugs for years, eventually causing a chemical imbalance. Some did it out of ignorance, while others did it to receive additional income. This causes them a host of problems once they become adults. This is cruel and unusual punishment, and it should be investigated.

Some sisters detest their children's father so much that they mentally or physically abuse them. They fill the children's heads with their hatred for their fathers in a way that if their fathers are incarcerated or suffer from substance abuse, they despise the children repeatedly comparing them. If they resemble the hated father, they can easily become victims of physical abuse. Some of these children eventually repeat the traits of their fallen fathers after years of being conditioned.

The virtuous black woman has been replaced with p-poppers, twerkers, thots, and bad bitches. Some sisters have no civility; they dress in revealing attire in places of worship, to a court, or even when applying for a job. Some of these outfits would make prostitutes feel ashamed. I'm not one to cast aspersions, but you can only come to one conclusion when you dress as inappropriate as some sisters. Sex appeal isn't just determined by the way you dress. There's plenty of sisters who are sexy that dress appropriately. Like it or not, the way you dress allows others to distinguish your character.

Social programs like welfare have historically encouraged black women to remain single. They disqualify any sister who is married or even in a relationship. Social workers would make random visits to investigate if a sister had a brother in the house? In the **1974** black cinema classic **"Claudine"** starring **Diahann Carroll** and **James Earl Jones,** this scene is carried out. Claudine Price is a mother of six who falls in love with Rupert Marshall, a sanitation worker. They want to get married, but that's complicated because she would get cut off welfare. His meager salary cannot support a wife and six children. The white social worker constantly stops by investigating if she's seeing a man or having items they considered contraband. What kind of social service would encourage this? Women on welfare cannot be in a relationship or own a new television? This permeated in sisters' minds; the remaining single became a benefit. This proves the government's complicity in destroying the black family.

In **1990 Sharazad Ali** sparked a lot of controversy after releasing her book, **"The Black Man's Guide To Understanding The Black Woman."** This book was a scathing expose on the behavior of black women. Sisters were upset with Mrs. Ali, accusing her of subjecting them to subservient roles. I think most of them were really upset with her for spilling the beans. The legitimacy of the issues she wrote about was ignored. Many women protested but never admitted to being that disrespectful or to the character traits she illustrated. Mrs. Ali should have been commended for her work. Her book should be used as a tool for self-examination. Authors like Alice Walker, Terry McMillan, and Toni Morrison are applauded for their works, which usually placate black women.

Many sisters are afraid of criticism, even if it's constructive. Their daughters learned this behavior and ended up with the same character flaws. Because there's no man in their lives, their sons grow up with ways and actions like females. He's sensitive, emotional, and latches on to his mother, who nurtures him like a baby. He won't entertain the thought of leaving home, clinging on to his mama way beyond his years. We call these types of brothers "momma's boys."

John Singleton made a movie about a brother like this. **Baby Boy** starred **Tyrese Gibson**, **Taraji P. Henson**, **Snoop Dog**, **A.J. Johnson,** and **Ving Rhames**. The movie was about the complicated relationship between Jody and his mother, Juanita. Juanita has enabled him, making him complacent. Conflict arises when she starts dating Melvin, who is recently released from prison. This makes Jody jealous because he's no longer getting all of his mother's attention. He initiates a dispute with Melvin that eventually finds him getting his ass kicked. Sisters bring their sons up like this, unknowingly setting themselves up for problems later.

Some sisters treat their sons like they are in a relationship with them. They encourage them to hustle in the streets to provide them with a good life-style or additional income. They stifle his development and sabotage his relationships with women. They fill him with guilt to persuade him to do anything they please. Some sisters believe they should be rewarded for being a mother, but no child asks to come into this world or choose their parents. Placing this amount of pressure on a child is extremely unfair. You can never repay someone for providing you with life. If every mother had a price tag, I doubt anyone would be wealthy.

Some sisters condone their children's unruly behavior then are filled with regret if they are murdered or imprisoned. With no man around, all of this was allowed to fester. They listened to **Destiny Child's** hit song **"Independent Woman"** then became inspired, although **Beyonce** sang of independence she is married.

Lots of black women admire **Michelle Obama**. Sisters love her, and she gets tons of compliments from them. They speak of how well she dresses, how intelligent she is and how well she represented the president. She's into physical fitness, loves working with children, and promotes healthy eating. These are the things that should be emulated by most sisters instead of the exploits of the Atlanta housewives. The women on reality shows have the means to take care of themselves. They are entertainers whose careers may even benefit from the negative attention. If caught in a tough situation, they can survive the damage to their reputation like Kim Kardashian.

That brings up another interesting issue. As a child, I was instructed never to bring home a white woman. Nothing draws the ire of a sister more than seeing a brother with a white girl. Let us take a deeper look into this situation. What are black women teaching their sons that make them shun sisters? What's making their sons want to run to women of other races? We cannot blame his father for this. Some sisters must be implanting that thought into some of these brothers' minds.

Unfortunately black people are viewed as a monolithic group; this is something I found to be a double standard. When A black person does something heinous, we all seem to feel the heat. Some of these traits are attributed to our tribal communal way of life before interacting with the Europeans. So when sisters act like this, it reflects upon them all. Most black women fail to speak out against sisters who behave like this. They give the impression that they find their behavior inexcusable yet acceptable. It's like there's a secret code among black women to show solidarity. Young sisters observe this and do the same.

I know that every black woman doesn't fit into every one of these categories. As I mentioned in the previous chapter, I am subjected to some of our behavior traits as a black man. Some black women must honestly see that they are subjected to some behavior traits that all black women share. It's not chauvinistic to require a sister to do what black women have done for our families for centuries.

There's no evidence that black men collectively mistreated their women or collectively held them back. So, therefore, black women did not need to join any feminist movement. If we had problems, we should have solved them among ourselves. I admit that the feminist movement bought attention to important social issues like rape, gender discrimination, and sexual harassment. The success of the women's movement is widely touted, while its negatives are never mentioned. The movement encouraged a lot of rouge behavior by women making some of them undesirable. **Jo Freeman, Naomi Weisstein,** and **Shulamith Firestone** ancestors were never enslaved or discriminated against like us. Under their leadership, sisters willingly weakened themselves and endangered their families. We have a habit of entrusting the same people that are historically untrustworthy. It's unwise to think that the founding members of these movements weren't crafting something that would eventually harm black women.

Racism white supremacy will always trump gender. I don't say this without facts to support it. After white men accepted their demands, did anyone think why they acquiesced? If some sisters can do it again, most would rethink their position, but there's no reset button the genie is out of the lamp. The younger sisters do offer the only hope we have to end this cycle. Without consciousness rap, all of this could have remained hidden. When **Public Enemy** titled their album **"Fear Of A Black Planet"** it got me thinking. I had to know why they would name their album that? I know they didn't name it that for any reason.

Rap music is often accused of being misogynistic, but those that feel this way never consider the experiences of these artists. It's conceivable there are women exactly like the ones these rappers talk about. Some sisters even adopted these demeaning titles; that's why female rap groups emerged like **HWA (Hoe's With an Attitude)** and **BWP (Bytches With Problems)**. I can imagine **Harriett Tubman** turning over in her grave if there is such a thing. If she were alive today, how many sisters would you think will feel the pellets of her shotgun?

The black woman is incredible, but she isn't without her flaws. The courts, educational and social systems have fooled some of them. I know sisters are smart enough to figure this out. A lot of you are beautiful, well educated, and successful. To the brothers reading this, sisters may have flaws, but we must not abandon them; we have flaws as well. Years of this behavior have created division, leaving most of our women and children alone. Grass root movements must be started by black women that deal with these issues. Agendas must be put in place to mend the relationships between us. Sisters must adopt realistic expectations of brothers. The sanitation worker, postman, mechanic, waiter, porter, construction worker, customer service representative, sales person, and laborer should be given the same consideration as the ballers.

"I think it's time to kill for our women. Time to heal our women, be real to our women and if we don't we'll have a race of babies, that will hate the ladies that make the babies." "Keep Ya Head Up" Tupac Shakur.

CHAPTER 9

THE HOUR OF CHAOS

"The people gotta pay a price for peace. If you dare to struggle you dare to win if you dare not to struggle then god dammit you don't deserve to win. Let me say peace to you if you're willing to fight for it." **Chairman Fred Hampton**.

Joining the Navy was eventful. I have already gone to the Philippines, Hong Kong, Guam, and Korea. I was stationed in Yokosuka, Japan, but getting there wasn't easy. When I first received them orders, I was upset. I couldn't believe they were trying to send me halfway around the world. I called my brother for advice. He advised me that I had the right to refuse those orders. Later that night, as laid in my rack, I really thought about that. I had to remind myself I specifically joined the Navy to travel. I realized I would be missing out on a great opportunity if I refused those orders, so I accepted them then prepared myself for Japan.

Shortly after that, on **October 17, 1989,** an earthquake registering **6.9** on the Richter scale rocked the bay area, killing 63 people. At the time, I had never been in such a catastrophic event like that. New Orleans has hurricanes with some occasional flooding when it rains but never did the ground move.

The earthquake occurred during the World Series. That season, the big game featured the **Oakland A's** vs. the **San Francisco Giants**. It was billed as the **"Bay Area Series."** The area was in turmoil; we were running around Treasure Island, helping to secure the base. We assisted in some rescue efforts in the community, helping to bring food, water, clothing, and medicine. With all this going on, my ship's out date was pushed back. I didn't make it to my duty station until more than two months after I was scheduled.

While I was in the Bay area, I saw some stuff I only read about in **Iceberg Slim's "Pimp"** or seen in movies like **"The Mack."** One night on the way back to the base, I fell asleep on the bus missing my stop. I ended up in a shady area of San Francisco, where I stumbled upon a track. A track is an area where Jon's, prostitutes, and pimps gather for business. I have never seen anything like this before so I stopped there for a while in awe. These were real pimps and hoes. It was an eye-opening experience. This confirmed to me that subculture existed. Anyone who proclaimed to be a pimp to me afterwards would have to show and prove.

The day I arrived in **Japan**, I experienced a culture shock. Until then, the only thing I knew about the Japanese was Ninja's, Godzilla, Samurai, and karate flicks. I expected to see the Japanese dressed as I did in the movies. I thought they walked around all day in kimonos and shit. To my surprise, they dressed like we did in America. They dressed like we did in the Hip Hop movement. They were wearing all the brands we wore, including starter jackets and **HBCU** gear. I knew they probably didn't know anything about these schools.

The evening we arrived, my man Robert and I decided to go out to the base club. Once I settled in, I realized they played rap music all over Japan. I went to clubs in **Tokyo, Yokohama, Negishi, Harajuku, Roppongi, Shinjuku, Sasebo, Okinawa** and **Zama**. They primarily played Hip Hop or rhythm and blues. In Tokyo, several clubs exclusively featured reggae, jazz, and funk. I was astonished by their love for black music and how far Hip Hop had traveled.

In **1991 Public Enemy** released their fourth full-length album, **"Apocalypse91' The Enemy Strikes Black."** The album featured songs like **"Can't Trust It," "Shut Em Down"** and **"By The Time I Get To Arizona."** By The Time I Get To Arizona was a song protesting the state of Arizona's refusal to make Martin Luther King Jr. 's birthday a holiday. Shut Em Down was a song suggesting what we should do to greedy companies that profit from the black community with no support. "Can't Trust It" was about black people trusting white people then being betrayed.

"So here's a song to the strong 'bout a shake of a snake and the smile went along with dat." "Can't Truss It" Public Enemy.

This song came full circle to me naively. I joined the military believing we wouldn't be in any conflicts. On **August 2, 1990,** the United States intervened in a dispute between **Kuwait** and **Iraq.** The U.S. sent troops to Kuwait, responding to Iraq's threats to invade the country. They called this conflict **"Operation Desert Storm."** This conflict lasted until **February** of **1991.** I was sent T.A.D (temporary assignment duty) from my ship to **Saudi Arabia** and the **U.A.E,** where I remained until it ended. This took me away from the security of my ship. My ship provided safety if we went to war. I was assigned to an aircraft carrier which offered even more pro-tection. They sent me to **Fujairah, Bahrain,** and **Jebel Ali,** and then I was assigned to **Riyadh.** I joined the Navy only to be under the supervision of a crazy Marine Gunnery Sergeant "can't trust it" yeah, right.

In **91,' Ice Cube** released **"Death Certificate,"** his most influential solo album, certainly his most conscious. This album was notable for the songs like **"Color Blind," "The Wrong Nigga To Fuck With,"** and **"No**

Vaseline," his scathing diss of **NWA**. Cube showcases incredible growth as an artist in recording another spectacular album that introduced Hip Hop to **Dr. Khalid Muhammad,** the national spokesman of the **Nation Of Islam**. His brilliant speeches are heard throughout the album, providing the narrative.

De La Soul released another classic album, **"De La Soul Is Dead."** This proved that they redefine themselves pushing rap beyond its boundaries. **DeLaSoul** was a trio out of **Long Island** that consisted of **Posdnuos, Trugoy (Dove),** and **DJ Maseo**. They break away from their so-called "Hip Hop hippie" image declaring the death of the daisy age.

A Tribe Call Quest dropped one of the best albums in the history of Hip Hop, **"The Low-End Theory."** Building on the success of their previous album, they cleverly produce an album with a creative blend of musical influences. This critically acclaimed album is still adored by many. It's regarded as one of the most creative rap albums ever produced. **Cypress Hill** breaks more stereotypes outta **South Gate, California. Sen Dog, B-Real** nasal flow and **Dj Muggs** production was a realistic look at life in the barrio. Their self-titled album was much needed in Hip Hop. Their single "How I Can Just Kill A Man" was huge, displaying another example of rap music's balance. The most compelling album to drop that year was **Tupac's** debut album **"2Pacalypse Now."** The album was perfectly blended with street vernacular, black empowerment, and political activism. Tupac Shakur is one of the most influential artists in the history of Hip Hop. Born in **New York,** Shakur first appeared in the game as a member of **Digital Underground**. His mother and stepfather were former **Black Panthers** or **Black Liberation Army** members. **Afeni Shakur** and his legendary stepfather **Mutulu Shakur** validated his roots in the black power movement. He revealed his revolutionary ideas in interviews or shared them in his music. Tupac embodied the spirit of empowerment; he was loved, feared, admired, respected, misunderstood, and hated by many. He influenced the Hip Hop community in a way no rap artist had ever done. On **"2Pacalypse Now"** he recorded songs about serious subjects like **"Brenda's Got A Baby."** This song was about a young girl who gets molested by her cousin. It's a socially conscious song that addresses an uncomfortable issue. There would be other great songs on the album like **"Souljah's Story," "If My Homie Calls,"** and **"Violent,"** but the most interesting song was **"Trapped."** Trapped was about a brother in prison having a conversation with his brother on the outside. Although he's in the belly, his man encourages him to remain positive.

"Naw they can't keep the black man down." "Trapped" Tupac.

Honestly, my first understanding of prison life was watching the movie **"Penitentiary."** Penitentiary was released in **1979**; it was written and directed by **Jamaa Fanakaa,** starring **Leon Issac Kennedy.** The film follows Martel Gordone, aka Too Sweet, who's wrongly convicted of murder. He's sent to serve his time in a prison somewhere in Arizona. On the night he arrives, he finds himself in a fight with his cellmate "Half Dead." The fight started when Half Dead attempted to assault him sexually. After a lengthy battle, Too Sweet emerges as the victor. Later on, he agrees to participate in an illegal boxing tournament run by the warden. The winner of the tournament would receive a full pardon. To train him, he enlisted help from his new cellmate, an older inmate named Hezekiah "Seldom Seen" Jackson. Most of the movie is focused on a homosexual culture that is allowed inside of this prison. It's never addressed neither by prison officials nor the inmates.

Angola Louisiana State Penitentiary has a history of these kinds of abuses. They named it Angola because the slaves who congregated in that part of Louisiana were from that part of Africa. **Angola** is located in **West Felicia parish,** about **150** miles from **New Orleans**. The prison spans over **18,000** acres with a farm that inmates work on daily. Regarded as one of America's most dangerous prisons, it houses some of Louisiana's most violent offenders. Most of the inmates in Angola probably will never be set free.

In **1971 Albert Woodfox** and **Herman Wallace** organized a protest against abuse by correctional officers in Angola. They were **Black Panthers** serving time in Angola for robbery. The two inmates demanded an immediate end to a culture of rape that dominated the prison. The Department Of Corrections wasn't pleased with them organizing for prison reform, so they became targets.

In **1972** they were convicted of the murder of correctional officer **Brent Miller** in what was described as a hit. All-white juries convicted both men in **St. Francisville Parish**. The evidence against them was based on testimony from inmates who were given lesser sentences for testifying against them. They were sentenced to life and a special form of Louisiana justice called CCR (closed-cell refinement). This meant they would be locked away from everyone in solitary confinement 23 hours a day. At around the same time, **Robert King,** another member of the **Black Panther Party,** served time in Orleans Parish Prison for robbery. In **1972** he was moved to Angola then charged in the conspiracy to kill officer Miller. At the time of the murder, Mr. King was locked up **150 miles** away. **June 10, 1973,** he was charged with accessory to murder when an inmate was killed on his tier. Prison officials charged him as an accessory even though the inmate responsible for the murder confessed. The guilty inmate testified he is the one who killed the man in self-defense in order not to implicate Mr. King. They both were convicted in a shady trial held in **St. Francisville** by an all-white jury. Mr. King was given the same sentence as Woodfox and Wallace joining them in CCR. They all remained in solitary confinement for **29 years;** collectively, they were known as the **Angola 3**.

This story is one of the biggest cases of injustice ever heard of in the United States. Faced with huge pressure from the community, including some in Congress, Mr. King was acquitted of accessory to murder then released. Mr. Wallace was eventually released when it was ruled that women had been excluded from the grand jury that charged him. On **October 1, 2013,** he was released from Angola to die three days later of liver cancer.

February 19, 2016, Albert Woodfox was released on his 69th birthday. He spent a historically long **44 years** in solitary confinement.

Sometimes when I called home, it made me depressed. I was always greeted with news of a childhood friend murdered or imprisoned. A lot of family and friends were incarcerated for various crimes. They were giving out time like it was water and nobody was thirsty.

"The nature of the criminal justice system has changed. It is no longer primarily concerned with the prevention and punishment of crime, but rather with the management and control of the dispossessed." "The New Jim Crow." Michele Alexander.

The war on drugs that President Reagan emphasized was a war on the Black community. Most drug offenders are prosecuted under some version of the **Rockefeller drug laws**. Former New York governor Nelson Rockefeller authored these laws. In **1974** Rockefeller was appointed vice president under Gerald Ford following the resignation of Richard Nixon. He had ambitions of being president, so he went through great lengths to appear tough on crime. Rockefeller's ideas were signed into law in **1973**.

The Rockefeller drug laws apply mandatory minimum sentences for small amounts of cocaine, marijuana, or heroin. The laws draw distinct punishment for certain forms of drugs like powder cocaine compared to rocks. There are severe sentences for rock cocaine even though both forms of the drug are the same. Data shows that certain groups of people are likely to have certain forms of drugs, i.e., whites powdered cocaine and blacks rocks. These laws give long sentences to non-violent offenders. Under **Bill Clinton,** they were federally mandated to make the prison population what it is today.

Black people struggle educationally, spiritually, mentally, physically, and financially. Community activists always talk about how poverty plays a role in the crime. The reality is unpopular, but the truth is indefensible. When there is an unfair proportion of wealth, people will do whatever possible they have to do to survive. As I mentioned earlier, the drug trade is risky, but it can be lucrative. The money made from selling drugs could provide instant finances. School is a better option, but it's a process and cannot provide immediately.

Many of our communities have been stripped of programs that offer alternatives. There's nothing for the youth to ascribe for. Some school district's athletic, fine arts, and music programs have been eliminated. These children have no way to nurture whatever talents they may possess. Most of them have a lot of free time on their hands, the perfect cocktail for mischief. This is all done by design destined them for street life.

The school system, the social system, and the judicial system all play a part in incarcerating blacks. It's been estimated that prison houses are built based on the test scores of third graders. The state of Louisiana houses the most prisoners globally, so what does that say about our 3rd-grade teachers? How can this be possible considering Louisiana is smaller than Texas, California, New York, Illinois, and Florida?

New Orleans survives primarily on money from tourism. According to the convention and visitors bureau, New Orleans makes approximately **7 billion** dollars annually from tourism alone. We host super bowls, the jazz festival, the Essence festival, and the French Quarter's festival. The city hosts conventions practically every day of the year, including some holidays. There's Mardi Gras, the Bayou Classic, NBA all-star games, and other events held annually. This type of economy creates the need for service-orientated workers. Restaurants and hotels are a vital part of this industry. New Orleans should have the best-paid hospitality employees globally, but they get paid slave wages. This is unfair, considering the work they do is vital to the economy of the state. Without the money generated in New Orleans, Louisiana couldn't survive. Some waiters, waitresses, and bartenders make great money from tips, but greedy restaurant and bar owners found ways to profit from that. The need to fill these low-wage positions is important because tourism is our main source of economy.

Louisiana provides the United States with huge amounts of oil from offshore rigs in the Gulf Of Mexico. Most of those dollars don't go to Louisiana, not to mention New Orleans, and this isn't comforting. The central business district, the French Quarters, and various parts of uptown are beautified to show the best of New Orleans. While the areas affected most by hurricane **Katrina** like **New Orleans East** and the **9th ward** are neglected.

Before the storm, the 9th ward boasted the highest percentage of black homeowners in New Orleans. Most of these homes had been in these families for decades. After tearing down the projects, most of those people were forced to live in this area. New Orleans East was once considered a great area for the black middle class. There were areas like East Over with multi-million-dollar homes. Some of these homes were owned by well-known celebrities and professional athletes. There were lots of privately owned businesses, shopping malls, and mega-churches. After Katrina, these neighborhoods were desolate, and the area became a food desert. All the little affordable housing was pushed out here.

When the projects were dismantled, the tenants were given promises of returning to the community. They promised them they would be included in the rebuilding process; however, many contractors hired undocumented workers paying them below value. Few minority contractors were hired, while out-of-state firms represented by Europeans got huge contracts. The money the government sent to rebuild New Orleans was sent to places in the state unaffected by the storm. After getting paid, some contractors did substandard work or left the job incomplete. Some homeowners were forced to pay back grants given to them by the government's faulty "Road

Home" program. A lot of promises were broken, leaving New Orleans with an identity crisis. Former New Orleans mayor **Ray Nagin** mentioned plans to gentrify New Orleans in his book **"Katrina Secrets."**

The minimum wage is always debated in congress, but they know it's a joke. It's not even a livable wage, everything has increased, but salaries have remained the same. The inequality of wealth in this country is alarming. The top **1%** is in control of most of the money. To most of them, the poor is seen as a nuisance. Some executives can make ten times the amount of the average worker. Students leave college every year under enormous debt. People purchase homes they know they can't afford. In most political races, the focus is primarily on the middle class. It's as if the poor don't matter or exist. This is why the lure of making slave wages fall short of the potential of making thousands a week.

New Orleans doesn't have a lot of manufacturing or tech jobs. They often go to people who live outside of the city when the few jobs in this industry become available. The present unemployment rate for black males in New Orleans is over 52%. This staggering statistic was presented during a debate in one of the recent mayoral races. Some college graduates from Louisiana have to endure these struggles, so they often accept jobs in other states. Outdated policies have crippled Louisiana, making the state look ignorant to people around the world. Those elected to serve Louisiana hinder us the most. If I were to document the amount of political misconduct, it would fill up the library.

In Louisiana, Sheriffs, judges and wardens are allowed to own for-profit prisons. It shouldn't be a surprise that they do all they can to keep their businesses thriving. How could this be in America, there are three branches of government to maintain democracy? These for-profit prisons owned by law enforcement agents are a direct conflict of interest. How can any judge or law enforcement officer be impartial especially when it might hurt their business? This system is ripe for corruption; it ruins people's lives and their families.

I consulted with ex-cons, who stated firmly without family help, they would be in dire straits. Imagine the stress associated with having a loved one in prison, especially if they are innocent. I understand that some people need to be locked away like violent or sexual offenders. Those types of criminals are a true danger to the community. I feel some white-collar criminals should be locked away too. Those types of criminals repeatedly destroy people's lives by deceiving them out of their pensions and retirement funds. It's been proven that we cannot arrest away the crime problem. Sheriffs and judges know this, but they continue to make a lot of felonious arrests. Some police chiefs give their officers quotas.

Wardens barter prisoners for work details, so this is a form of slave trading. They're for profits; prisons offer no chance for an inmate to learn a trade or further their education. This limits any hope of rehabilitation. They wish to continue this cycle to keep their businesses thriving. Americans should be in outrage that this is allowed. The reason there's no outrage in America is that Caucasians aren't affected. In every part of society, when white people are affected, change ensues. Black people aren't different from any other Americans. We desire a good life and are not afraid to work for it. I bet no white person on the planet would change positions with us. Poverty often leads to desperation. Nobody turns to crime just for the sake of it. The average European never considers this, nor do they care. Some racism is learned behavior, but much of it is institutionalized. Most white people are afraid to face these realities because of the scrutiny it would bring upon them and their forefathers. I'm not making excuses for criminals; I'm only outlining the factors behind why they do the crime. This dichotomy is often ignored. Until wealth is distributed equally, crime is going to be an issue.

The department of education administers these so-called standardized tests. Students who score poorly on these tests are held back. These tests are usually given to 4th, 8th, and 12th graders. The tests are unfair; they don't consider cultural differences, schools' lack of resources, unqualified teachers, and the environment. It has a negative impact that could lead them to become uninterested in education. Imagine having to pass a test that they fail to prepare you for. Think of the humiliation of being in class with people younger than you because you failed this one test. I even heard of some valedictorians failing these exams. Some students have lost academic scholarships. State-run schools require these tests; some charter and private schools aren't required to give them.

Charter schools are really private schools run with public money. Most charters have their own set of requirements independent of the state. Charters are often run by people with little to no experience in education. Most of them aren't interested in working with the children they serve. The school is treated like a business, not an institution for learning. Some of these so-called educators run these schools like prisons or detention centers. Most teachers in charters are unqualified or come from programs like Teach For America. Teach for America offers incentives to teach like helping to pay students loans and also guaranteed teaching contracts. The program sounds great, except the people who sign up aren't always into education. Some only come into the program for the incentives then become overwhelmed with the job. Programs like this lead to disgruntled non-compassionate teachers. There have been many documented cases like this where teachers abuse children. Keep in mind these are the people we trust our children with. What happens to children at these ages can affect them for the rest of their lives.

Children will search for love even if they find it in the wrong places. They look for answers from their parents, but they are often products of the same environment. With all things considered, it all seems like a trap. That's ironic "a trap" is what they call a drug house in the hood. It's a catch-22 if you choose higher education because you will graduate with a lot of debt? If you chose a regular job or a trade, you would be a paycheck slave? If you hustle in the streets, you jeopardize your life or your freedom? What's troubling is that a lot of brothers choose the latter.

Some brothers are systematically controlled; they seem to function better when they are incarcerated. They have become so embedded with prison life to the point that they find it normal. They are part of a social-economic class beneath the underbelly of the United States. As a felon, you are prevented from living in public housing, cannot receive public or social assistance, are disqualified from Pell Grants or student loans, and cannot vote. I understand that you are a product of the decisions you make in life, but punishing someone forever is fundamentally wrong. It's unfair when they already served time for their transgressions. How can anyone survive under these types of conditions? That person's options are limited to the streets, and it eventually leads back to prison; it's a cycle.

Some brothers are blessed to find employment or go to school despite their criminal records. Most of them will tell you it's an uphill battle while emphasizing it's not for the weak; however, these occurrences are more of the exception. These are the kind of conditions you expect to hear from a third-world country, not in America. Prisons all over America are filled with non-violent offenders. Most of them were given plea bargains under tremendous threats of prosecution. Consider how many innocent people languish behind bars because of unscrupulous prosecutors. Most inmates cannot afford to defend themselves properly. The threat of prison doesn't deter crime regardless of how many prison houses they have erected. It's a social-economic problem. Until that issue is resolved, crime will continue.

Unfair laws like three strikes have guaranteed a healthy prison population. I recall a story about a brother who stole a doughnut. This theft was his "3rd strike," so he was sentenced to **35 years**. A man's crime should fit his punishment. 35 years is unfair for an 85 cent doughnut. **Bill Clinton's** tough-on- crime policies have harmed people's lives. I'm sure some people thought he had great intentions. I understand everyone desires a safe place to live; however, many important points were overlooked.

Prison life is a world unto its own ruled by the most powerful inmates. Allegiances are the only way to survive, so some inmates become members of gangs or cliques. Extortion is acceptable, and inmates used it often. Prison rules are adopted in every correctional facility violators are punished severely. Inmates remain under stress; being around criminals every day can have that effect on a man. Some inmates have scars from confrontations with adversaries. The only comfort they have is an occasional visit from family or friends, letters, or call home. Most of their items are bartered for cigarettes are a huge commodity. This culture of life can become habitual considering how many years a brother spends incarcerated. Drugs are just as available in prison as they are on the streets—this offers little chance of rehabilitation for addicts.

Prisons are like universities of crime; most cats go in only to come out as improved criminals. Some brothers sensationalize the penitentiary; they eagerly share all their experiences. To them, prison is worn like a badge of honor. Some of these stories rival veterans who fought in combat. This neo-slavery mentality is translated to our youth making prison life acceptable.

"If you can control a man's thinking you do not have to worry about his actions. When you determine what a man shall think you do not have to concern yourself about what he will do" "The Mis Education Of The Negro." George Washington Carver.

The prison most difficult to escape for most of us is the one placed on our minds. Black people must recognize how mentally incarcerated we are. Our conservative values can be more dangerous than those of the European. We must allow time to dictate our agenda; we can no longer look at the traditional ways of doing things. We must have growth on all fronts, including our mentality.

Caucasians are constantly looking for ways to survive. Some of them are looking to live on the Moon if that meant getting away from us. We assist them in all their endeavors while ignoring our own. I will talk more about this in the next chapter.

We are some of the hardest headed people when addressing this subject. We adopted everything fed to us by the Europeans. We accepted their hero's as ours while allowing them to make ours into demagogues. We can't put all the blame on the European we had great leaders since the days of **Marcus Garvey**. Their ideas were often met with opposition by the same people they were trying to save. The same black people willingly accepted the Caucasian's ideology without question. The same thing happened to **The Honorable Elijah Muhammad, Malcolm X,** and **Nobel Drew Ali**.

How did we become so brainwashed to believe that the European care to teach us the truth? They have been lying to us from the beginning. We criticize each other sometimes as a means to satisfy the Europeans. We discreetly speak when discussing Caucasian's even in private. We are afraid to confront them even when we are within our rights.

The European really has done a number on us. They took away everything that made us who we were, replacing it with a doctrine of racism white supremacy. **The Honorable Elijah Muhammad, Malcolm X, Minister Louis Farrakhan, Cheikh Ante Diop, J.A. Rodgers, Dr. Khalid Muhammad, Dr. John Henri Clark, Bobby Hemmitt, Dr. Yosef Ben-Jochannan, Dr. Umar Johnson, Dr. Phil Valentine,** and **Tariq Nasheed** have all debunked European ideology. Still, many of us cannot break away from European mind control. All of these brothers were labeled militants, which meant they were crazy to most black people.

The **Willie Lynch** doctrine is a letter thought to be written by the historical slave master. The doctrine gives details on how to physically and mentally "make a slave." He emphasized if used properly, this method could be used to control their slaves for **300 years**. The authenticity of this doctrine has been up for debate; however, the results aren't.

Historically we have achieved far greater than the Caucasian. Our **400 years** of free labor were the foundation that built this country. Reparations should serve as restitution, but some of the biggest critics against reparations are some of our own. They cite some ridiculous reasons behind their opposition. We fail to see the tremendous power we have as a group. We use self-demeaning analogies without carefully examining their meanings like comparing ourselves to crabs in a barrel. If crabs were placed in a barrel, of course, they would claw and crawl over each other to escape. Crabs live in the water; a barrel is not their natural habitat. We place all the focus on the crabs' behavior instead of how they got into the barrel.

Some black people are accused of being "sell-outs," but how can anyone be a sell- out if they never sold in? Many blacks who are accused of such fit that description. Slavery was abolished over **150 years ago,** yet the chains remain on our brains.

"The chain remains until we uprise. Stuck in a land where we ain't meant to survive." "The Chain Remains." Naughty By Nature.

The oppressor removed their hoods then replaced them with suits. They came among us to continue their assault this time on our minds. Some of us know little about our ancestors but can tell you everything about the Europeans. We implore each other to conform; believing that would bring us rewards, but acting other than yourself will only take you so far. Those we choose to lead us decided to promote the same values as the oppressors taking their followers with them. They lie dormant as our communities suffer while the adorned Caucasian communities thrive. We value their friendship. Some of us have an insatiable urge to be among them. I'm not going to say that there are no white people I'm cool with. I served with some in the Navy. I just don't need them as friends to validate me.

Malcolm X had a young white student ask him, "What can she do to help the plight of black people in America?" His reply to her was nothing leaving her disappointed. In his memoirs, he said he regretted telling her that. I understand why he felt that way. A man of his stature surely could have used this young lady. Here's my recommendation to any white person if you're genuinely not a racist, you should organize like-minded Caucasian's then form an organization. The organization should address the behavior of other Europeans. You must work to eradicate the institution of racism white supremacy. Your coalition should force Congress to change the laws that unfairly incarcerated black people. It would help if you rallied against police brutality then lobby for reparations. This may not pay us back for everything your ancestors have done to us, but it would be a tremendous show of good faith. The United States sends billions to countries hit hard by atrocities or countries they support in wars. They surely can find money in the budget for reparations they have for others.

By the time **92** rolled in, I had already started the process of breaking the mental chains of racism white supremacy. I needed to release myself from the shackles mentally, physically, and spiritually. I started a healthy diet then I submerged myself into black culture. We have to devise a plan to detour our young men from both prisons mentally and physically. Even though the odds are against us, we must not be moved. We must put pressure on our elected officials to change these racist laws. We must run those out of office who are unwilling to make this commitment. We must realize that the legal system is not in our favor; it's a web of confusion designed to entrap you. Some of us must admit to being mentally enslaved, similar to a drug addict or an alcoholic, and then find a way to bring about healing. Knowledge your wisdom to understand your culture, then refine yourself so that you won't be a savage in pursuit of happiness.

"Cold sweating as I dwell in my cell. How long has it been they got me sitting in the state pen. I gotta get out, but that thought was thought before I contemplated a plan on the cell floor."

"Black Steel In The Hour Of Chaos," Public Enemy.

CHAPTER 10

STRICTLY BUSINESS

"Total chaos, no mass confusion. Rhymes so hypnotizing known to cause an illusion. Like a magician who pulls a rabbit out a hat son. I pull them all like a .44 magnum" "Strictly Business" EPMD.

It's **1993,** and by now, I had visited **Australia, Thailand, Indonesia, Malaysia,** and **India.** I found out that the world was a ghetto, as stated by a group named **WAR.** How ironic. In every country, there was a section for the dispossessed. I must have a ghetto magnet because everywhere I went, I encountered places like that. It wasn't uncommon to see them dressed like us with rap music blasting through every speaker. As a black man, I was treated quite well, and some countries embraced black culture to the point that it overwhelmed me.

Hip Hop had become larger than anyone had anticipated. Then we learned that **Dr. Dre,** the talented producer behind **Ruthless Records,** left the label behind a financial dispute. Another member of **NWA** was leaving, claiming he was unfairly compensated. This was beginning to look like a pattern. I know groups often break up but having members leave citing the same reason is more than coincidental. The **D.O.C** and **Michelle Le'** were also part of the exit. **Eazy E** is on record stating **Priority Records** executives played a role in influencing his artist. He mentioned the conditions of Dr. Dre's release was a percentage of his royalties from **"The Chronic."**

Has money come between the boys from the hood? We know money can play a role in a group breakup. This often happens in the music business; maybe we thought better of rap artists. Rap music had become **strictly business**. The Hip Hop community has to realize that now.

In **91'** Eazy E was solicited by the **Republicans** to become a member of the party. **Texas Senator Bill Graham** sent invitations out to people they recruited to join the Republican Inner Circle. The event was a fundraiser where President **George H.W. Bush** would be speaking. The media said he was sent the invitation in error, although nobody made any attempts to correct it. He attended the event that cost everyone $1,250. The publicity generated from attending the event was well worth the money he spent. Was Eazy attempting to sell out, or was he just being a good businessman?

In **1989 De La Soul** was sued by **The Turtles** for sampling their song **"You Showed Me."** The lawsuit was eventually settled out of court for a reported **1.7 million** dollars. In **91' Cold Chilling Records** was successfully sued over **Biz Markie** sampling **Gilbert O'Sullivan "Alone Again."** This was a landmark case before this ruling; samples didn't need to be cleared—this benefitted publishing companies who were now able to collect a lot of money. Rap labels now had to pay to clear samples. Biz Markie's album containing the uncleared sample **"I Need A Haircut"** was pulled from circulation.

Rick Grant, a member of the DJ crew, **Nu Sounds** overrode a toggle switch on a conventional DJ mixer. This small alteration created the crossfader. The improvement to this piece of equipment would make the crossfader a major component of rap music. Mr. Grant doesn't own the patent to this, nor has he received any recognition. DJs Like **Grandmaster Flowers, King Charles, Pete DJ Jones, Infinity Sounds** and **Cipher Sounds** made custom sound sets that major companies replicated. Rap music had become a money-making machine, and everyone was trying to profit.

When rap was introduced, it was viewed as a novelty. Most record executives thought it wouldn't last, assuming it would eventually go away. Like jazz and disco, they saw no value in it, but everyone wanted to profit when it defied the odds. The same way they did both of those genres.

November 12, 1990, Frank Farian, a music producer out of **Germany**, confessed that **Milli Vanilli**, a group he constructed, was a fraud. Milli Vanilli was a pop group, but Hip Hop influenced their music. Farian admitted that the group featuring **Rob Pilatus** and **Fab Morvan** of Munich, Germany, were not the actual singers behind their multi-platinum album **"Girl You Know It's True."** He revealed he used session singers actually to record the album. He recruited Morvan and Pilatus, believing them to be more marketable than the middle age singers who recorded the album. They were immediately dropped from **Arista** then forced to return the **Grammy** they won. Was Farian trying to deceive the listening audience or was he just being a good businessman? Was it all **strictly business**? Over the years, a long list of studio gangsters and pimps has been exposed as disingenuous.

Do rappers that promote negative images ever consider how they affect children? Parents should emphasize to their children that rappers are just entertainers trying to make a living. It's **strictly a business**.

"It's like a friendship and a business partnership. We have to always be conscious of the difference between them; because you know, some things can happen that will ruin one or the other" "B.I. Vs. Friendship" Gangstarr.

1993 was the year of **"The Chronic"** after his release from **Ruthless Dr. Dre,** and **Marion "Suge" Knight** established **Death Row Records.** Dr. Dre brilliantly produces a heavy funk influenced rap album. It was a distinctively creative new style of rap music he called **"G-Funk."** The album featured an impressive roster of up-and-coming rappers like **Snoop Doggy Dogg, The Dogg Pound, RBX, Nate Dogg, Warren G,** and **The Lady Of Rage**. No rap album ever sounded like this. It was innovative and extremely creative. The genius of Dr. Dre shines on songs like **"Let Me Ride," "Nothing But A G Thing,"** and **"Fuck With Dre Day."** Dre Day was a scathing diss, with Dre aiming at all his adversaries. The album's high point was **Snoop Dogg;** his chemistry with Dr. Dre made this album a classic. Out of **Long Beach, California,** his charismatic flow carries the album. This album was significant, and it marked a turning point in rap music. The influence of this album would be felt in Hip Hop until this day.

Greedy executives started encouraging their artists to produce tracks similarly. Everyone was trying to capitalize off this new sound. That resulted in tons of wack recordings. A few artists were successful, while the rest filed the airwaves with sloppy copycat material. This started the demise of the conscious rap era.

Record companies started looking for a marketable artist who represented "the streets." The content of the music was causality to the profits. The lyrics became degrading while sales soared. Rap artists became agents of the same devils they shun. The promise of wealth led more rap artists to alter their content.

While this was going on, some black CEOs had some control of the industry. Record executives like **Sean "P Diddy" Combs, Percy "Master P" Miller, Bryan "Baby" Williams,** and **Jermaine Dupre** signed lucrative distribution deals. The content of the music stayed the same, although these powerful black men had a lot of influence.

The music business replaced the DJ, the most important component of Hip Hop. Until then, every rapper had been attributed to a DJ. Companies were looking for any way to maximize profits, and the DJ became expendable. Most of them will tell you this was **strictly business**. This is one of the main reasons that rap music has suffered. The rapper gets most of the attention, but the DJ has always been the creative force behind him. No matter how much these companies manipulate their artist into recording negative content. It doesn't matter how many children are negatively influenced. The bottom line to them is the presidents.

Should we place all the blame on the music executives? As I mentioned earlier when discussing disco, the artist should demand more creative control. The consumer determines the market for any product, including music. With the sales generated, it's obvious they like this product. This tells me a lot about the people that listen to this music. It's kind of hard to imagine considering rap roots.

Even though rap music was changing, **1993** was a great year for rap. **A Tribe Called Quest** released their third full-length album, **"Midnight Marauders."** The Tribe improved their winning formula while producing another great album. **De La Soul** released arguably their best album **"Buhloone Mind State."** De La's brand of Hip Hop is showcased with a high level of maturity. They shine on songs like **"Breakadawn," "Ego Trippin Part 2,"** and **"I Am I Be."** **Digable Planets** came out of **Brooklyn** on fire; this smooth ass group consisted of **Ladybug Mecca, Doodlebug,** and **Butterfly**. Their critically acclaimed debut album, **"Reaching,"** garnered major recognition. It was a rebirth of the cool. **Jam Master Jay** released **Onyx's** debut album, **"Bacdafucup,"** on his **JMJ** record label. Onyx is an extremely hardcore rap group from **South Jamaica Queens** that consisted of **Sticky Fingaz, Fredro Starr, Sonny Seeza,** and **Big DS**. They all sported bald heads and rapped very aggressively.

KRS-One released his first official solo album, **"Return Of The Boom Bap."** He enlisted legendary producers **DJ Premiere, Showbiz,** and **DJ**

Kid Capri, then recorded another stellar album. **Tupac Shakur's** much anticipated sophomore album **"Strictly 4 My N.I.G.G.A.Z"** is released. The album was pushed back by his record label for months. Controversy arose when Vice President Dan Quayle suggested pulling **"2pacalypse Now,"** claiming the album influenced the killer of a Texas state trooper. Allegedly the shooter in this incident was listening to the album at the time of the murder. Tupac, not one to be silent, addresses Vice President Quayle throughout the album. This album gave us great songs like **"Holla If You Hear Me," "I Get Around," "Representing 93'"** and **"Keep Your Head Up."**

Eight ball And MJG come out of the south on fire with their debut album **"Coming Out Hard."** Coming from **Memphis, Tennessee** they release an album of content-rich in street vernacular. This allowed us to hear from an area that the Hip Hop community heard little from. **Black Moon "Enta The Stage"** was a prerequisite of what we would hear from a talented group of Mc's called **"The Boot Camp Clik."**

The most impressive album released that year was **Wu-Tang Clan "Enter the Wu-Tang: 36 Chambers."** Coming out of **Staten Island (Shaolin),** this mega rap group consisted of **Rza, Gza, Old Dirty Bastard, Inspector Deck, Method Man, Masta Killa, U God, Cappadonna, Ghostface Killah,** and **Raekwon The Chef.** These extremely gifted MCs redefine this era of Hip Hop. They influenced a host of rappers to follow while creating a movement. The Rza's unique production set this group apart from their contemporaries. Their gritty form of rap reestablishes Hip Hop roots while cleverly infusing consciousness. They enjoyed greater success as solo artists, music producers, fashion designers, business people, A&Rs, label executives, actors, and directors. Most of the Wu-Tang Clan are **Five Percenters.** Known also as the **Nation Of Gods And Earths.**

The **5%** is an extension group that was influenced by the teachings of **Nation Of Islam.** The Nation was founded in **1964** by **Allah,** aka **Clarence 13x.**

Members of the nation affectionately refer to him as **The Father**. We teach that **The Black Man is God** and **The Black Woman is The Earth**. They are studious astute brothers and sisters in the nation who fluently study **120 degrees**. 120 is the set of lessons they apply to their behavior. The Father dedicated his life towards educating the youth. He established a street academy for the youth on **125th street** in **Harlem**. He did tremendous work in the community providing a father figure for much-disenfranchised youths. He forged personal relationships with the people of Harlem. **New York** mayor **John Lindsay** often consulted with him on matters involving the community. On **June 13, 1969**, the Father was assassinated in the **Stephen Foster** housing projects; his murder remains unsolved.

The 5% influence on Hip Hop culture is well documented. Terms used in rap like **"dropping bombs"**, **"word is bond,"** and **"the cipher"** derive from their teachings. Members of the Nation include **Rakim Allah, Big Daddy Kane, The World Famous Supreme Team, The Poor Righteous Teachers, Brand Nubians, Lakim Shabazz, Just-Ice, Busta Rhymes, King Sun, AZ, Guru, Digable Planets, Sunz Of Man,** and **The Gravediggaz.**

Guru of **Gangstarr** released the first of his **Jazzmatazz** compilations. These albums were a refreshing blend of Hip Hop and jazz. Perfectly arranged Guru records with an impressive list of musicians featuring **Lonnie Liston Smith, Branford Marsalis, Ronny Jordan, Donald Byrd, Roy Ayers, Carleen Anderson,** and **N'Dea Davenport**. He dared to reach back into the roots of black music marrying the two genres together perfectly. This project was tailor-made for him displaying his range as a rap artist. Jazzmatazz showed the world the depths that rap music can go.

I knew once **93** was over, rap music would never be the same. Money had changed the game. Rap artists had no limit to what they would do to get paid. To confirm this, ten years later, **50 cent** released his debut album **"Get Rich Or Die Trying."** Out of **South Jamaica Queens**, 50 cent would set another standard in rap music. His meteoric rise started with selling crack on the streets of New York. Like **Tupac,** his legend rose after surviving an attempt on his life. Some rappers attempted to copy these circumstances. Shit like this became **strictly business**. Many rappers have died trying without getting rich, leaving their families grieving. What is **strictly business** to record labels is a catastrophe to us.

With all the money made, music executives can wield tremendous influence if they desired. CEOs could clean up this industry overnight if they cared to. This serves as evidence that money is not their only motivation. Let's take a look at a rap artist career that mirrors a pro athlete. Similar to pro athletes, most rap artists don't make as much money as some people assume. Just like a pro athlete, many artists enter the industry at a young age. Not accustomed to having huge amounts of money, they irresponsibly spend it all. Rap artist contracts allowed deductions for plenty of expenses. They get paid once all these expenses are covered, often leaving them with little. This is why there's desperation to make hit records.

A successful rap artist establishes a certain lifestyle. They would do anything to remain in that lifestyle, even if it means recording degrading content. In the movie **"The Five Heartbeats,"** one group member stated, "cross over ain't nothing but a double-cross." He said this in frustration after the record label changed their album cover. Once most rappers lose their core fans, their careers are never the same. Often the momentum is lost, which is very important in Hip Hop.

These days the media gives you more access to celebrities' lives than ever. Imagine what it must be like being a struggling rap artist watching a less talented rapper display his nice house on **MTV Cribs**. Think of what it may feel like seeing wack rappers flashing wads of cash showing off their nice cars, money, and jewelry. It's a difficult situation; after all, nobody gets in the music business to be broke.

Some rappers' only motivation is money, even if their music contributes to a nation of dummies. Since **93'** most rap artists have adopted a gangsta persona. This seems to be a requirement in rap music. Today's listeners wouldn't accept rappers like **The Fresh Prince, Heavy D, PM Dawn, Kwame, Monie Love, MC Hammer,** or **Young MC.** With all the gangsters in rap music, why haven't they taken over the industry? This is common practice to those in the underworld. Some of these so-called gangsters leave or get released by their labels then complain of not getting paid. This is confusing because all the gangsters I knew wouldn't allow that to happen. This should serve as an example; it's all **strictly business.**

What's astounding is most consumers of rap are young white people. It's an eye-opening revelation. I bet some of you didn't know that. So these white executives want us portrayed in this manner? They are willing to pay millions to see us act a damn fool. Maybe this is the reason why the content has suffered? The great content of rap was forced underground. It became unpopular to promote consciousness in rap music. Record companies these days are unwilling to promote any conscious rap artist. Rappers like **Dead Prez, Black Starr, The Roots, Truth Universal, NJeri Earth, Jasiri X, Aiesha Sekhmet,** and **Narubi Selah** would have been huge stars in the '80s. This issue is a microcosm of the problems we have when it comes to business.

According to the recent census, there are approximately **1.9 million** black-owned businesses in America. They estimate that these businesses generate around **1.3 billion** dollars. The National Association of Black Accountants estimates that black people spend **1.1 trillion** dollars in this country. That's nothing compared to how much money we spend. This is the result of integration which weakened us economically. The only real black conglomerates are in the entertainment industry, so-called civil rights leaders, or mega church pastors.

We have been taught that white businesses are better. Self-hatred plays a part in why we don't support our own people, even knowing that Ice isn't any colder coming from a white business owner. We don't support black businesses for some of the most asinine reasons. I've had plenty of black people tell me how much they distrust black business owners. For some of them, one bad experience is all it took. They levy some of the same complaints against white businesses, but they continue to support them. The way some of us treat black businesses is very disrespectful. It's not uncommon for some blacks to go into a black business to barter for unreasonable discounts or renege on a service agreement. The same people would dare to do that to a white business. Most of the businesses we support have roots in discrimination; some didn't serve us before integration. Some of these businesses even have roots in slave trading.

With the staggering economic power we possessed, we could solve many of our problems if we grouped our economics. We can use our economic power to effect social change. Just a one-day boycott would cripple a lot of these businesses.

At one time, all we had were black businesses. In my neighborhood, we had **Mr. Dan's, Wills game room, Tenie Weenie's, Split Seconds, Mrs. Lou's grocery, Alexis Fried Chicken, Bus stop po boys, Masons Motels, The Gallo movie theater,** and **Jumping Jimmy records.** This was as recently as the late '80s. **The US government** played a role in destroying many black businesses as well. Check the history of every urban area; there was a thriving black community in each one of them. Most of them were destroyed when the government used eminent domain laws to construct interstates highways through the middle of them. Many of these business owners were given unfair market prices for their properties or had them taken away.

Black businesses need our support more than Wal- mart, Sam's, or Costco's. In the '80s, fashion designer **Gloria Vanderbilt** stated she didn't design her high- priced jeans for black women. The moment she said that, every black woman should have stopped buying her clothes. In the **'90s, Tommy**

Hilfiger stated he didn't appreciate his brand being so closely linked to Hip Hop. This statement didn't stop blacks from buying his clothes. We always make white business owners rich, and then they tell us how they really feel about us.

The fashion industry is a hot spot for racism white supremacy. Black models struggle daily to get top jobs in this industry. This is because the fashion industry only recognizes white standards of beauty. I read an article recently about a black model that came under fire behind her full lips. This is a feature almost exclusive to black women. Some white women try to imitate these features by injecting their lips with dangerous chemicals. It's hypocritical because white women with full lips like Angelina Jolie are considered sexy. Black women are known for having big butts. **Serena Williams** is an elite tennis player; she has won **22 tennis titles**, including victories at **Wimbledon, The French Open, The US Open**, and **TheAustralian Open**. She's physically fit and one of the finest black women on the planet. She's constantly body- shamed in the media, mainly for her buttocks, but the same hypocritical media adores Kim Kardashian's.

As a black business owner, you must present your businesses in the best manner possible, providing excellent service. Employees of black businesses must maintain a high level of professionalism. The same professionalism they would have if they were working for a white business owner. Service cannot be undercut because of the people you work for or serve. Black business owners should remove employees unwilling to make this commitment. Black businesses have to adopt the same attitudes as their counterparts and stay competitive. They must provide an advertising budget to get their ads out to their target consumers.

Some in the community expect black businesses to put back into the community. I understand this concept; however, how can they put anything back in if they aren't successful? Nobody goes into business to be broke.

I saw a news report out of **Rochester NY;** black people were upset with Popeye's chicken. While running a special sale, Popeyes ran out of chicken. People were on the news saying how they traveled to several Popeyes locations looking for chicken. Some of them were so upset they called Popeyes corporate office to complain. I know somewhere in that town there was a black-owned restaurant that served fried chicken. I bet most of them don't rush out to vote or involve themselves in their children's education like they did for that chicken.

We trust white business owners so much that we pay almost whatever they charge. I know it's impossible for us to find alternatives because they cornered the market. The few black businesses around should be supported, even if that means going out your way. It's not uncommon for people of other nationalities to do this. The most successful businesses in the community have to stop being the churches.

As I conclude, I want to say I wrote this book out of my love for Hip Hop. I wanted to demonstrate how Hip Hop provided direction to a lost generation. There are books written on Hip Hop but not many on the individual impact it played in our lives. I wanted to debunk the theory that rap music never contributed anything positive.

I honor those that gave us some direction. We were a lost generation searching for the right way. Some rappers today avoid that responsibility while the ones of my era embraced it. To all of the artists mentioned in this book, I salute you. The jewels you dropped ended up being valuable. They became the cornerstones towards a lot of us getting knowledge of self. It's never been stated how a few words from these gifted artists saved lives.

To my mentors, thank you for caring enough to dedicate your time. I appreciate all your efforts in making us productive members of society. **Vice,** this book should serve as evidence that your work in raising me to be a righteous man didn't go in vain. **Roosevelt** rests in paradise big brother. **Patrick,** remember you accompanied me to most of these historical rap shows. To my beautiful children **Khadijah** and **Zaire,** this book serves as evidence that I cared enough for our people to speak truth to power. I love you.

PEACE !!!

Thank you for reading my book. If you enjoyed reading this book, please leave a review on Amazon. I read every review and they help new people discover my books.

Peace and Infinite Blessings
Firstborn Malik

ABOUT THE AUTHOR

Firstborn Malik is a father, a member of Allah's Five Percent. A veteran of the US Navy, A social and political activist an emcee, and a music producer. His knowledge of music and black culture started as a youth born and raised in New Orleans, Louisiana. Raised uptown in the Calliope projects helped to build his relationship with the community. This relationship served as the landscape to write How Hip Hop Helped To Raise A Generation. The depth of his travels helped to develop more information about black culture as viewed by the world. A product of the New Orleans public school system helped to enlighten him on the miscues of the educational system.

CPSIA information can be obtained
at www.ICGtesting.com
Printed in the USA
LVHW010719060621
689465LV00011B/407